KU-328-848

BLOODY IRISH

Celtic Vampire Legends

Dr Bob Curran comes from Co Down, Northern Ireland. He travelled the world before gaining degrees in History and English, and a Doctorate in Educational Psychology. Dr Bob is a broadcaster, most recently working with the BBC. He serves on cross-border cultural bodies and develops historical tours all over Ireland. Dr Bob lives in Coleraine, Co Derry, with his school-teacher wife and family.

To my children, Michael and Jennifer, and to Mary, my long-suffering wife, for all their love, patience, interest and support during the writing of this book.

BLOODY IRISH

Celtic Vampire Legends

BOB CURRAN

MERLIN

PUBLISHING

Published in 2002 by
Merlin Publishing
16 Upper Pembroke Street
Dublin 2
Ireland

www.merlin-publishing.com

Text Copyright © 2002 Bob Curran
Arrangement and Design Copyright © 2002 Merlin
Publishing

ISBN 1-903582-19-9

A CIP catalogue record for this book is available from the
British Library.

*All characters and events and places referred to in the
book are fictitious and are not intended to refer to any
person living or dead and that any such reference is
coincidental and unintentional.*

Typeset by Gough Typesetting Services
Printed by Cox and Wyman Limited, Reading

All rights reserved. No part of this publication may be
reproduced, transmitted, or stored in a retrieval system of
any kind without the permission of the publisher.

CAVAN COUNTY LIBRARY
ACC No C/255883
CLASS NO. 398.21 UK
INVOICE NO. 7263
PRICE £9.60

Cavan County Library
Withdrawn Stock

CONTENTS

Cavan County Library
Withdrawn Stock

INTRODUCTION

Vampire! The very word conjures up visions of eerie East European mountains; of deep, near-impenetrable forests; of crumbling castles where blood-sucking Balkan nobility dwell; of Slavic peasants huddled in their villages under a sinister Transylvanian moon. And yet, the oldest recorded vampire story comes from Ireland. *The Legend of Abhartach* has its origins in North Derry and may have served as at least partial inspiration for the epitome of all the vampire-kind – Dracula himself. And, when you come to think of it, the two greatest writers of vampire tales – Bram Stoker (*Dracula*, 1897) and Sheridan Le Fanu (*Carmilla*, 1872) – were both Irishmen. Almost every culture in the world has its vampires – the Malay *penanggal*, the Filipino *aswang*, the Albanian *sampiro*, the 'clinging souls' of Talmudic lore, even the Brazilian *jaracaca* – but, arguably, nowhere does the belief have more imminence than in Ireland.

Death, for the ancient Celts, held a slightly different emphasis than it does in the modern world. Rather than being 'the end of all things', it was a transition period from one sphere of existence into another, and the dead still maintained contact, in some form or other, with the world that they had left. Undoubtedly, this notion had its origins in ancient ancestor-worship, when it was believed that the dead kept a protective watch over their descendants.

It was also believed that from time to time the dead returned in order to warn, to punish, to advise and to receive some form of recompense for their continued protection. It was a fundamental tenet of Celtic belief that, at certain times of the year, the veil between our own world and the next was so thin that the dead could and did cross from their own bleak world and visit the places they had known when alive. Here, they could enjoy all the pleasures of which they had partaken during their lifetimes – a pipe, strong drink, a hot meal. And they could visit their descendants, who were, in turn, obliged to provide these comforts for them.

One of the nights when the walking dead crossed from one realm to the other was the festival of the *Fáilte na Marbh* (the Feast of the Dead) on 31 October, now celebrated as Hallowe'en. This period was regarded as an almost mystical time, when all manner of magic and sorceries abounded; but it was the returning dead who preoccupied the common mind, and tokens and foodstuffs were left out for them. Even within recent memory, old women in the Mourne Mountains of County Down would scatter the *gleeshins* (ashes and residue) of the fire on the hearthstone during Hallows' Eve night, and if these were disturbed they knew that their ancestors had been back and had been sitting by the fireside during the hours of darkness.

As Christianity crept slowly across Ireland, old beliefs began to change. This is not to suggest that they disappeared – far from it – but simply that they were modified in order to fit in with the new ethos. Ancient superstitions that had existed since pagan times suddenly became the stated orthodoxy of the Christian religion. Pagan wells, for example, became holy wells, and their allegedly miraculous properties, formerly attributed to gods and spirits, were now ascribed to the power of saints; pre-Christian shrines became sites of sacred pilgrimage; festivals celebrating non-Christian deities were changed so that they celebrated Christian feast-days or the lives of national or local saints. One of these festivals was the *Fáilte na Marbh*.

The early Christian Church embraced the notion of the

returning dead with a certain degree of enthusiasm. Indeed, part of its teaching was that, at times like Hallowe'en, those who had 'died in Christ' were permitted to return for a night in order to visit their loved ones and to be 'entertained' by them. The Irish Church also sometimes gave a moral perspective to such returns: for instance, it was said that 'a woman who died leaving a newborn child or a man who died owing money would never rest quiet in the grave' – stressing the values of motherhood and of settling one's debts. I can remember an old woman who, as a baby, was said to have been suckled by a corpse (that of her mother, who had died in childbirth) and through this had acquired the 'power' to cure ringworm in humans.

However, it was the 'entertaining' of these returning dead that often concentrated the minds of the living. After a year or so in the cold grave, the dead expected to sit at the firesides of their descendants and be warmed, fed and tended. Old mountain folk in County Down sometimes left a glass of whiskey and a piece of bread (later shortbread or cake) on the hearthstone 'for the dead'. This was usually gone in the morning (although other members of the household may have had something to do with the disappearance). Some of the departed, nevertheless, were more forward and were not content with a sup of whiskey or a scrap of cake. Some of them chose to arrive at the evening mealtime to have their food with the rest of the family. And, after years in the grave, such cadavers were not easily fed! There are many tales (some of them humorous) regarding certain families' anxiety, as Hallowe'en approached, that their dead relatives would eat them out of house and home! To refuse these dead ancestors the hospitality they demanded was to invite their wrath, their curse and usually supernatural harm as well.

One such story concerns a man whose aged mother-in-law lived with him and his family. There are many versions of the tale, but this particular one comes from the slopes of

Knocklayd, near Ballycastle in County Antrim. In this story, not only was the old woman incredibly bad-tempered; she was also extremely greedy, especially when it came to food. As the poor man's family grew, the strains on his resources became more pronounced, particularly with a gluttonous old relative to support. Each day, the old crone would eat bacon, yellow meal, bread, eggs, sweet milk, buttermilk, bits of beef, porridge, stews and soups in vast quantities. The poor man's heart was nearly broken, and he was more than grateful when at last the old beldam died. At last, the greatest drain on his resources was over.

But he was wrong. As the family sat down to a meal one evening, the latch of the door was lifted and in came the old mother-in-law, fresh from the grave, to take her accustomed place at the table. The family was obliged to feed her. And if she could eat when she was alive, she ate more when she was dead! She ate bacon, potatoes, yellow meal, bits of beef, potato bread, wheaten bread, soda bread, stew, soup, sweet milk and buttermilk, eggs and turnips – all in even greater quantities – washing it all down with beer and several glasses of whiskey 'for the warmth'. When she had finished, she rose from the table and went back to the grave, while the family breathed a collective sigh of relief. But the next night she was back, demanding the same sustenance, which her son-in-law had to provide. There was a distinct danger that he would go bankrupt from the food bill alone! In the end, the family had to bring in a local priest to exorcise the greedy corpse and send her back to the grave, from where she troubled them no more.

Such stories, while usually humorous, had a dark and sinister side as well. It was widely believed that if the descendants of any of these walking cadavers had been negligent in their duties – if they had no food, if they had not said the requisite Masses for the repose of the soul – then the corpse had the right to punish them. If food was not provided, the corpse might take blood as a substitute. This belief was linked to very old superstitions.

The importance of blood – both animal and human – has been recognised since earliest times. The Celts viewed it as a revitaliser, a regenerator, a restorative. In the winter months, when the ground was hard and cold with frost, it was thought that libations of blood would bring back heat and vitality to the soil. Consequently, the earliest Celts may have practised human sacrifice, spilling their most precious substance on the sterile earth in an attempt to bring it back to life. Only then would the crops grow again and Nature burst forth – it took blood to kick-start the process, so to speak. Something of that idea may have transferred itself into the notion of the blood-drinking dead. If no food had been laid out for the returning corpse, then it was entitled to turn upon members of its own family in order to gain some sustenance and to restore the warmth to its body after a period in the cold clay. Usually it was only the blood of either domestic animals or near relatives that this 'vampire' took, but sometimes it ventured into the wider community to slake its unnatural thirst.

For the Christians, human blood frequently drew demons to it. Undoubtedly, in many ancient cultures, the spilling of human blood had been central to the worship of old, pre-Christian gods. These pagan rituals had been discouraged by the spreading Church, and many of the gods who had received this tribute were translated into awful demons in Christian eyes. Those things that consumed blood – such as the *crom cruach* (a fertility god, to whom a blood sacrifice appears to have been made each year) – were now considered to be agents of evil. Vampires had become things to be feared, rather than being simply the revenants of respected ancestors. The tales about them acquired a sinister and terrifying aspect. Who knew what lay out there in the cold darkness? Undoubtedly it was the hostile dead, who chose to work evil against the living. This was the basis for such stories as *Dracula,* the classic vampire yarn.

It has been argued by many literary experts that the first

section of *Dracula* is more Irish than East European. The imagery of the narrow coach-roads with their roadside shrines, the gothic mansions and the peasants making obeisance reflects less of Transylvania (a country to which Stoker had never been) and more of the Ireland he knew. Indeed, it is further argued that the novel reflects much of the horror of nineteenth-century Ireland in its preoccupation with the questions of land, aristocracy, hardship and death. It was written in a time when one of the greatest horrors ever to hit Ireland – the Great Potato Famine of 1845–1852 – was still uppermost in the common mind. And here, too, is a connection with blood. As food stocks dwindled and the Irish people experienced disease and emaciation, they began to draw their sustenance from other sources – sometimes from the blood of domestic animals, cattle in particular. Blood-letting at certain sites (which still bear names associated with blood and slaughter) rapidly became a common practice, and 'relish cakes' (blood mixed with a handful of oatmeal or yellow meal and vegetable residue and cooked in the style of black puddings) became well known in some areas.

This must have made an important impact upon the Irish psyche and may well have strengthened the folkloric image of the blood-drinking dead. The tales about them took on a much more sinister and darkly supernatural tone, linked with misery and death.

It was not only human blood, however, that some of these animated cadavers sought from the living, but 'vital fluids' and energies as well. Here they shared similarities with the *succubi* of ancient Rome and the *aswang* of the Philippines, which drew 'bodily essences' from those whom they attacked (usually as their victims slept). Their attentions were used to explain lethargy and bouts of physical weakness in warriors and leaders. Ancient Irish kings and heroes were said to have been beset during the night by such demons, who drained them of their prowess (either through nocturnal sexual intercourse or by other means) and left them withered and exhausted husks. This was reputedly one of the attributes of the Lenahaun Shee (the fairy mistress), who drained poets and chieftains of their vitality and then discarded them. The notion of being 'drained' has often more to do with the loss of vitality than with the obvious loss of blood.

Which brings us to the present collection of stories. All of them are Irish or have an Irish connection, and while not all of them are strictly true, they all contain an element of the darker folklore of the Irish countryside. All of them have primarily rural settings, some have religious connections – and this is not surprising: in Ireland, the land, the community, religion and death are often inextricably linked. The majority of them are based on old stories that I have heard up and down the country – demonstrating that, while the vampire does not feature prominently in formal Irish literature, the blood-drinking dead nevertheless appear in Irish folklore. Some deal with the conventional blood-drinking vampire, others with the spirit or demon that drains energy and all that is good from the body. In most of the tales, true locations and proper names have been disguised, and some of the facts have been modified for various reasons. They all may have some base in reality, and they all may reflect older beliefs than we can presently understand. Read them and make of them what you will.

Do vampires exist, then? And, more importantly from our point of view, do they exist in Ireland? Gloomy landscapes, ruined churches and lone trees arguably seem to be far more sinister here than they are anywhere else. And of course the countryside is soaked in a long and bloody history. Can we truthfully say that there is not *something* lurking out there in the darkness of the Irish night? Nobody knows for certain; but as you read these tales, especially if you read them in Ireland, take a look over your shoulder. The undead may be closer than you think!

Bob Curran
Coleraine, January 2002

CAVAN COUNTY LIBRARY

'And where are you going today?' Mrs O'Dwyer refilled his teacup and set it gently back on the edge of the large breakfast table, ignoring the maps that had been haphazardly spread out across its surface.

Redmond looked up from his study, keeping his finger on a specific area of the locality. Lifting the cup, he took a long sip and moved the finger across the contours in front of him.

'Oh, I thought I'd take this road to Drumechtry – isn't there an old church there that's worth seeing?'

The landlady nodded enthusiastically. 'Indeed, Mr Redmond, I've heard it said that there's been a church at Drumechtry since the earliest times. There was a grand professor from London stayed here one time, and he said that there'd been worship there ever since the fifth century. He said that there was a great abbey there at one time. Sure, isn't the Blessed Saint Murchu buried there?' She lowered her voice slightly, though there was nobody to hear. 'During the Penal times it was a wonderful place for worship out of the way of the authorities. It was said that if one of the pagan English ever set foot in its grounds, they'd be fried by hellfire!'

Redmond smiled ruefully. 'I'll have to watch myself, then,' he said.

Mrs O'Dwyer raised a hand to her mouth in alarm. 'Oh! Savin' your pardon, Mr Redmond. I didn't mean any harm – you bein' English an' all. No offence to you, sir!'

John Redmond laughed. 'None taken,' he replied, and turned his attention back to his maps. 'And from Drumechtry,

I thought I'd take this road' – he traced the course with his finger – 'across the hills to Roughfort and Ardnahannon. From there, I'd take the main road round the edge of Lough Maul into Barnesmore and back here again.'

Mrs O'Dwyer nodded approvingly. 'Ah, there's plenty to see at Roughfort,' she agreed. 'There's an old church-tower that was demolished when Black Cromwell's troops fired a cannonball at it –'

Redmond laughed. 'That story must be told about every church in Ireland,' he said. 'As well as the tale about Cromwell riding his horse up the nave and spitting in the baptismal font. I've heard it so many times, it's almost unbelievable!'

Mrs O'Dwyer looked a little nonplussed. 'But in this case it's true, sir! He burned Roughfort almost completely!' she protested.

Redmond decided not to pursue the matter. He ran his finger along another section of the map. 'There are a couple of roads over the hills I could take,' he observed.

Mrs O'Dwyer smiled. 'Ah, the hills are lovely at this time of the year. Not so nice in the wintertime – covered in mists and rain – but now they're at their finest.'

Redmond wasn't really listening; his eye had settled on something on the map.

'There's a road here that runs through a place called Castlequinn,' he said. 'It seems to be a shorter way than the one through Ardnahannon.'

Mrs O'Dwyer's expression flickered, but the smile was only gone for a moment.

'There's a beautiful High Cross at Ardnahannon,' she continued, as if she hadn't heard him. 'Raised by the Culdees, who had a holy house there. It's really worth seeing, Mr Redmond, indeed it is.'

'I see that there are the ruins of an old Norman castle down at Castlequinn,' he persisted, squinting at his maps.

The landlady shook her head, as if trying to clear it of

some vague but unpleasant odour. 'Only a few old stones in among the grasses. You could walk past it and see nothing.' She hesitated. 'And there's nothing else at Castlequinn, either – just a few old ruined cottages. The village was abandoned years ago. The Great Hunger finished it, but some people stayed on until they could stay no longer.' Her voice lowered. 'It always had a bad name about it in the countryside.'

Redmond nodded. He knew that the Famine had devastated many small villages in this part of Galway beyond any recovery. All that was left were the names on old maps. Yet the notion that people had continued to live in Castlequinn, long after the Famine had destroyed the place, intrigued him a little. For a student of history, it might be worth visiting a Famine village.

'How long did people continue to live there after the Famine?' he asked.

Mrs O'Dwyer pulled a face. 'Oh, long years. But there's nothing to see there at all. When I was a girl, the castle was just an old hump of a place, covered in grass and ivy; the local farmers had carried most of it away to build their barns and outhouses – dressed stone, you see. I think there's nothing left to see but an old well. Like I said, you'd miss it from the road. There's a far better castle at Barnesmore.'

Redmond sipped thoughtfully at his tea. He wasn't at all convinced.

'Is there a church at Castlequinn?' he enquired. 'One that served the castle?'

Mrs O'Dwyer sniffed. 'There used to be one,' she replied. 'But, like the castle, it's fallen down long ago.' She hesitated. 'I wouldn't go anywhere near Castlequinn. There's far more to see at Ardnahannon and Barnesmore. Much prettier places, too.'

Redmond shrugged and finished his tea. 'Maybe you're right,' he admitted. Mrs O'Dwyer seemed pleased with herself; she poured him another cup and bustled away, while her guest mapped out a route to Ardnahannon.

And yet the mention of the rotting Famine village wouldn't leave his mind. Back in his room above the pub, as he prepared for his day's walk, he dragged out his large and detailed gazetteer and almost unconsciously turned its pages. The book seemed to fall open of its own volition. Redmond stopped and read:

> CASTLEQUINN: *Village situated around the remnants of a minor castle, reputedly built in 1184 by a Norman noble, Simon de Senlis. Although de Senlis spent little time there – he joined and fought in the Third Crusade – the keep was occupied by his confessor, one Adam Lennox, an eccentric cleric of dubious repute who was suspected of being a warlock. It is said that Lennox raised evil spirits several times in the castle and in a small church nearby. The church is long gone; as early as the late 1400s, it was recorded as being 'in a ruinous state', and no trace of it now remains. During the sixteenth century the castle was a fortress of a sept of the O'Choinns (O'Quinns), from whom the village takes its name. It was the principal stronghold of Tadhg Dall (Blind Tadhg) O'Choinn, who com-mitted great atrocities against his enemies and prisoners. Tadhg Dall was killed in 1538 by his illegitimate half-brother Fergananam ('fear gan ainm' means 'man without a name' – in other words, 'illegitimate man'), who, according to legend, led a party of men into the castle using a secret passage and repeatedly stabbed the blind man as he sat at his fireside. Two years later Fergananam himself was slain by the Fitzgerald Earl of Desmond, who stormed and captured the castle in 1540. In 1570, the lands and village were given to Sir Thomas Bewley as part of the*

Plantation settlement. The Bewleys were absentee landlords, but the village continued until it was almost destroyed by the Irish Potato Famine in 1847. During the Famine years the castle itself was demolished and used for stone by locals, and little trace of it remains today. Even after the worst effects of the Hunger, a few hardy souls continued to live there until the turn of the present century. Only some dilapidated ruins of the village exist today.

That was all, though there were several pages on Ardnahannon and Barnesmore. Redmond closed the gazetteer. Mrs O'Dwyer had been right: not really much to see, and it certainly wasn't worth varying his route to go there. The walk across the hills to Ardnahannon would be pleasant.

✢

Indeed, the day was very pleasant. Under an azure sky, the upland scrubs and heathers covered the ground in a rich carpet of blossom and gave the breeze a faint, sweetish scent. The air was breathtakingly clear, and from the heights over which he passed, Redmond thought he could almost see the distant ocean, miles and miles away. He could certainly see the waters of Lough Maul as they caught the sun in the west. Houses were few and far between, and much of the land was open and empty moorland, haunted only by birdsong and sheep. And in this entire and wonderful wilderness, he met few people, for the roads were almost deserted. Those he did meet simply gave him a greeting and passed him by. It was exactly as he wanted it. The stresses and strains of the teaching profession melted away under the rising sun, and the curious, slightly academic boy that John Redmond had once been began to emerge once again into its light.

A stressful year lecturing on history at a college in the

north of England had left him exhausted and on the edge of what he assumed was a nervous breakdown. He had been, his doctor had hinted, as close to emotional collapse as he would want to come; better to get away for a time and rebuild his shattered nerves. This was what he needed, he told himself – some time in his own company on the remote Galway hills. He watched a hare start across a wide space on the hillside, and a scattering of magpies as they landed on the road a good way in front of him. It was what he wanted, after months in the close, intense atmosphere of the college: simply to get away from it all and wander aimlessly through the Galway hills, soaking up the peaceful atmosphere and getting rid of the inherent poisons of urban life.

He had seen the ruined church at Drumechtry – in truth, there wasn't much to see, just a piece of a gable wall with what had once been a window in it – and a small holy well that was supposed to cure goitre. Then he had set out across the uplands to look at the ancient, historic and extremely ornate (so his gazetteer told him) High Cross outside Ardnahannon village. He moved the knapsack in which Mrs O'Dwyer had packed his lunch a little further up his back, and marched on down the road.

Halfway along the narrow road that wound down to Ardnahannon, a ruined Celtic cross stood on the other side of a shallow ditch, close to the roadside. Shrines and crosses were common in this area of Ireland, and Redmond viewed it with little surprise. Nevertheless, he paused and leapt across the ditch to look at it, for its base seemed to be elaborately carved. He need not have wasted his time: the hill winds and rough weather had taken their toll on the stonework, and most of the carvings and illustrations were now indecipherable.

With a grunt, he turned back to the road; but, as he did so, something else caught his eye. Tucked away amongst the long roadside grasses were the remnants of what appeared to be a fallen fingerpost. Like the base of the cross, it seemed to have worn away; it lay on one side, still showing the way that it had been pointing. Pulling back the grasses, Redmond looked down at it. The pointing finger only contained one word, in stark, dark letters: 'Castlequinn'. Turning, Redmond saw an even narrower tarmac road leading down the hill off to his left, winding round a corner and out of sight.

'It seems I'm forever destined to be shown the road to Castlequinn,' he observed with a slight laugh. Somewhere in the upland emptiness around him, a crow answered his humour with a loud, raucous cry. 'All roads lead to the damned place.'

He leapt back across the ditch, intending to turn down the road towards Ardnahnnon; but, almost unconsciously, he took the road to the left, down the twisting slope towards Castlequinn.

Around several turns of the road there was a cottage – a long, grey-stone building with a peaked roof hanging down over its doorway like a frowning brow. It was tucked so tightly into the base of a slope that it seemed to be part of the hillside itself. Narrow windows squinted at Redmond as he passed, like eyes set in a wizened grey face. As he drew level with it, the peeling door opened and an old woman looked out. She was almost skeletal, her tufts of white hair poking out from under a workman's battered hat, her body swathed in layers of clothing that ranged from a torn grey jumper to a filthy plaid skirt and heavy dark wellingtons. A pipe was crammed into one corner of her mouth.

'It's a fine day,' Redmond greeted her civilly.

She fixed him with what seemed to be a hostile gaze. 'It's not often I see people on this road,' she snapped back, in a sharp, high voice that reminded Redmond of the crow he'd heard earlier. 'Nobody ever comes along this road any more.' And she took another step beyond the doorway.

Redmond paused in his stride. 'Nobody goes to Castlequinn?' he asked cheerily.

She came a little way down towards the side of the road.

He saw that her thin, weather-beaten face seemed to be slightly twisted, as if from an ancient stroke, and that the pupil of one eye was obscured by a translucent film.

'Not since Finucane put the gate across the road to the village. He says it's part of his land and he doesn't want people walking through it.' Taking the pipe from her mouth, she spat angrily onto the ground. 'Bad cess to him and his family. They're a dark brood, true enough!'

Redmond was a little taken aback by her vehemence. 'I'd thought that I might go down and see the castle,' he told her. 'But if the road's closed off ...'

She sidled up towards him, and even in the open he caught a whiff of her body odour. 'The castle's gone. There's nothing to see – not even stones. It was Finucane and his father – aye, and his grandfather afore them all. They carted it all away for building, stone by stone. No good'll come of what they did. That was the castle where Black Lennox lived, and his curse is on it. That's why they never prospered. I know, for Finucane's been my landlord for many's a long year, and he's never prospered on my money, anyway. The crowd of them's always been poor. Land's poor, people's poor, village is in ruins.' Redmond was beginning to suspect that the old creature's mind was more than a little unhinged. 'But you go down there an' see for yourself, sir. See what Finucane did to the village. His grandfather bought it from old Miss Bewley, you know. Ah, the Bewleys – they were a dark people too. Never cared much for their tenants. Same as Finucane and his dark crew.'

Redmond was rapidly becoming unsettled by her ramblings, which no longer seemed to be directed at him.

'There's nobody living in Castlequinn now?' he asked, backing away down the road.

She laughed – a high, cackling sound that did nothing to relieve his disquiet. 'Not a one! The Bewleys drove 'em all off. And Finucane's grandfather did the rest. Ye'll have heard of him, no doubt – old Pat Finucane, a black-hearted villain if ever there was one. Known the length and breadth of the country for his wickedness!'

Redmond wanted to hurry on and get out of her presence. He backed further away, but, hobbling forward, she made to follow him. He was sorry that he'd come along this road.

'I wish you well on your journey, sir,' she said. 'But if I were you, I'd turn back up the road and go to Ardnahannon. There's only Black Lennox's place down there, and a few stones of the O'Choinns'. A big family they were in this area, sir – big and bloody. There's an old well down there where they say Blind Tadhg drowned his baby son. Only six months old, I'm told. Imagine that, sir – drowned him in a well.' Again her tone had taken on an air of vague abstraction, as though her mind was incapable of holding a thought for too long.

Redmond kept easing back from her, hardly realising that he was moving further and further back down the roadway. In the end the old woman turned away and went hobbling back towards her house. 'That's all there is to see, sir,' she called after him. 'If you see Finucane, tell him you've been warned about him. Tell him Annie Sullivan warned you. A dark man, sir. He never got the good of the money that he took from me. A dark man indeed.' She stood in the centre of the road, watching Redmond warily as he backed further away from her. 'If you see Finucane, ask him about Foley!' she called after him, and laughed a little unpleasantly.

Redmond hoped she would go back into her house, but she showed no sign of moving. At last he turned and walked onwards, down the slope towards Castlequinn.

A little beyond the old woman's house, the tarmac road gave way to peat and grass, and Redmond found himself following a path that was little more than a country track. Obviously nobody had travelled this way for many a long day. The path twisted and turned, winding downwards, round bends, until the old woman's house was lost to view and only the high slope swept down to the side of the road. On the other side of the path, the land fell away into a narrow gully. A couple of times Redmond thought about going back up the hill, but the thought of having to meet the crazy old woman again prevented him. Better to go down and see what Castlequinn looked like.

Rounding a bend near the bottom of the hill, he saw the first signs of the village. It lay in a hollow. On either side, the hills rose steeply upward, then curled around behind Castlequinn as if to shut it away from the outside world; a wide ditch surmounted by a high thorn hedge scrambled up the slopes on either side of the peat track, reinforcing the isolation. A large five-barred gate hung across Redmond's path between concrete posts. Above it, a lone tree spread long branches that overhung the gate, throwing it into shadow.

And beyond this, in the midday sun, was the gable-end of a low stone cottage, half-covered with ivy and creepers. The road passed by this dwelling and turned sharply to the right, where Redmond could see a number of other buildings – mostly cottages, some with slated roofs, some open to the sky. All seemed to be made of stone and looked fairly sturdy. He also glimpsed the edge of some larger building on the far side of the cottages; it looked like a church of some kind. And behind all this, the land rose steeply again to form a small plateau, on which he assumed the castle had once stood.

He walked on to the gate and looked across into Castlequinn. A few straggly-looking sheep moved among the buildings, but apart from these the place was deserted. He made to lay a hand on the topmost bar of the gate, and drew back suddenly. The entire bar was covered in a thick skein of barbed wire.

'This Finucane certainly doesn't want people trespassing on his land!' Redmond said softly to himself. A crow – perhaps the same bird he had heard earlier – called harshly from the heights above him, but other than that the day was still. Redmond looked around, unsure of how to proceed. Should he go back up the hill and leave the village behind? But his historian's instincts urged him to try to find a way over the gate and explore the falling houses.

Suddenly he spotted a narrow gap between the great overhanging tree and the concrete post from which the gate was suspended. With a minimal effort, it might be possible to squeeze through. Redmond tried it – even though he had to remove his knapsack momentarily – and, a few breathless moments later, stood on the other side of the gate. Castlequinn lay in front of him.

After the effort of pushing through the gap, there was relatively little to see in the deserted village. Most of the buildings had been demolished, either deliberately or by the elements, and only gable walls and ruined doorways revealed where they had once stood. Many of them had no roofs; their slates had apparently been removed, and the birds came and went through the skeletal rafters. Even those cottages that remained relatively intact were in a sorry state. Glassless windows peered uncomprehendingly, like blind eyes; thorns waved from among the broken stonework.

Redmond poked about among the traces of a vanished people. The interior of a roofless dwelling by the side of the turf road held only a thick carpet of nettles and tall, waving weeds, with the framework of an old chair poking up from the middle. Sheep wandered everywhere, aimlessly chomping at grass or peering out of ruined doorways. Redmond ducked to avoid a trailing briar that hung from a fallen wall. His foot noisily collided with a rusting kettle that someone had thrown away, and around a corner he came on the headboard of a long-gone bedstead, propped against the wall of a cottage.

But a couple of cottages remained more or less intact, and it was to one of these that Redmond went to explore further. This building was tucked in at the point where the road swung off to the right, up towards the small church-like structure (which now looked as if it might once have been a school) and the height on which the castle had probably once stood. The cottage – a low, single-storey dwelling – varied little from the others, except that it had once been limewashed, in contrast to the grey stones around it; now a dirty green moss had gathered across the whitish stone like a foul disease. A solitary sheep watched Redmond mournfully. Ducking through the low door, he stepped into interior darkness.

Because there was still a roof on the building, little light penetrated the inside. A few strands of sunlight coming through two narrow windows – one in the wall and one high up in the gable – turned an almost impenetrable darkness into a kind of smoky gloom and let him see at least a little of the room around him. He was standing in what appeared to be a large kitchen. A peeling door led to another room, but it was firmly closed and Redmond could see no latch to open it. Sunlight crept across stone flags towards him, and slowly, as his eyes became accustomed to the half-light, he began to pick out some features – a yawning fireplace with a great stone chimney-breast and a wooden mantelpiece; a discarded china jug under one of the narrow windows; a broken wooden chair pushed to one side of the chimney.

That was all; and yet he was sure that there was more. He had an odd feeling about the place – an inexplicable sensation that it had recently been inhabited and that the occupant had simply stepped out or passed through the closed door into another room. He had the distinct impression that if he were to turn suddenly he would see someone standing just behind him, someone who had been desperately trying to keep out of sight. There seemed to be a faint sound in the air, apparently amplified by the closeness of his surroundings – a vague murmuring, like people talking a great distance away. There were no discernible words, just the sensation of sound, and he put it down to the heat of the day and a minor stirring of the blood in his ears.

His sturdy walking boots rang on the flagstoned floor as

he moved forward towards the large, empty fireplace. As the sunlight fell against the crumbling stonework, Redmond noticed a strange discoloration on the wall to the right of the fireplace. At first he thought it was his own shadow, caught in a freak ray of light from the window; but then he realised that it couldn't be – it was far too small, hunched over on itself, and Redmond was tall and upright. Maybe it was some sort of lichen sprouting from the ancient stone, giving it a slightly darker tinge, Redmond told himself. And yet, in the poor light, he wasn't altogether sure. Maybe it was a staining of the very stone itself.

He moved forward and, stretching out his hand, touched the dark patch on the stone. Placing his palm against the shadow, he found that it was remarkably cold, even though it lay almost directly in the sunlight. As he touched it, he thought that the dark patch writhed and moved a little, as if it were folding in on itself; but that must have been a trick of the poor light. He felt a slight momentary sharpness, like the brush of a rough piece of stone; a thrill like an electric shock passed along his arm and jerked his entire body.

The sensation lasted only for a moment and then was gone, leaving only the muttering sound singing in Redmond's ears. He shook his head to clear it, and the sound slowly faded away. The half-gloom of the cottage swam oppressively around him and he felt his stomach turn. Dashing to the door, he tried to throw up; but, although his stomach heaved, he wasn't sick. He simply stood retching into a laurel bush for a moment, until his body settled and the day steadied around him. He leaned back against the cottage wall and rubbed the sweat from his face with one hand.

It was only then that he noticed his palm was covered in blood. A few red drops fell into the laurel bush. Damn! thought Redmond. He must have cut it on the roughness on the cottage wall.

Taking off the knapsack, he hunted in it for the paper

towels that Mrs O'Dwyer had put there with some sandwiches. A few dabs with these, and the blood was gone, although a little still welled from a minor cut just below the base of his thumb. He sucked at it, hoping it wasn't infected with the dirt from the cottage. Hadn't the old woman said that there was a well nearby? Maybe he could wash it there – if he could find it.

Leaving the cottage doorway, he walked up the grass-covered street towards the rise. Ruined cottages watched him as he passed them, their doors like gaping mouths, staggered that a stranger should be so bold as to visit Castlequinn. As the street opened up in front of him, he saw that the far end had been sealed off by a thick fence of barbed wire, reinforced with clumps of brushwood and scrub to form a barrier over which he doubted he could climb. Beyond this lay the rise up to the small plateau above the village, where he suspected that the well might lie.

Approaching the obstacle, he could see that there was no way round it and no way out of the village.

'Finucane again!' he muttered to himself. 'He mustn't want anybody in his precious village!'

Looking down at his hand, half-bandaged with the paper towels, he saw that the flow of blood seemed to have more or less stopped, although a few tiny red pearls were still visible. Maybe there was water somewhere else – a trough or something left for the sheep – in which he could wash it. He scanned the surrounding street but saw nothing. A low building to his left looked as if it might once have been a shop of some sort – its now-empty front window was much bigger than those of its neighbours – but it was mostly in ruins, and there was no water-trough anywhere close by.

As he moved towards the church-like structure, however, he was suddenly aware of a movement at one of its windows. A pale, narrow face looked out, then darted away into the interior of the building. Although he only had a glimpse of the

watcher, Redmond had the impression of a youngish man –
and, by the furtive, shambling movement, one whose wits were
not completely together.

For a second Redmond stood there, unsure what to do.
Then a voice split the silence of the early afternoon, making
him jump.

'Ha! I see you, Foley, you devil!' The voice was certainly
that of a young man, but it was pitched in an odd way, almost
girlish in its tone. The accent, too, was awkward and heavy,
with some kind of local emphasis that made it almost
impossible to follow – almost, but not quite. It came again
from the church-like building, the emptiness of the place giving
it a kind of echo. 'I see you! Ha! You devil! I see you!'

Redmond took a few steps forward; as he did so, a fallen
slate half-hidden among the grasses cracked under his foot
like a pistol shot. 'Ha! You think you can creep up on me,
Foley?' shouted the voice. 'I'm wise to your tricks. Ha! You
devil!' And once again Redmond saw the pallid, pasty face
move across the gaping window and duck down behind the
wall of the structure.

'Hello?' he called. 'Who are you?'

'Ha! You devil! Ho! You devil!' the voice replied; and
suddenly a figure streaked from around the corner of the
building, almost cannoning into Redmond in its frantic rush.
He had the impression of dark hair, heavy dark clothes, and
that same pasty face he had seen at the window. The being
went barrelling past him, and Redmond had to leap aside to
avoid being hurled to the ground. Even so, the stranger struck
him a glancing blow on the side before disappearing into the
falling doorway of a nearby ruin. 'Ha! Foley! You thought I
didn't know you,' the words came drifting back. 'But I know
you, you spawn of Black Lennox. I knew you by your crooked
finger and the hanging nail. Ho! Foley! You devil!' And it was
gone.

Redmond didn't know what to make of it, but a definite

unease stole up on him. Here he was, practically trapped in a
deserted village with someone whose wits were clearly astray
– someone who, he suspected, might have the phenomenal
strength of the weak-minded – someone who might even kill
him in this remote place. It was a kind of nightmare.

'Hello?' He tried to get some grip on the situation. 'Hello?'

The empty houses rang with an unearthly, high-pitched
laughter as the unseen youngster roared his mirth from
somewhere close by.

'You thought you were safe in your corner beside the fire,
did you?' he shrieked. 'Ho! You devil! Devil Foley!'

The voice was drawing further away, and at last Redmond
found the courage to step into the ruined doorway through
which the stranger had vanished. There was nothing there
except a wide expanse of grass and weeds, flanked by falling
walls. The back of the dwelling had tumbled down, and beyond
it lay a tangle of low bushes and long briars, sheltered by a
steep slope into which a muddy track disappeared.

This was clearly where the other had gone, but Redmond
didn't feel inclined to follow. The encounter had unnerved
him a little.

Shivering slightly and still nursing his injured hand, he
turned away and headed back towards the gateway through
which he had entered the dilapidated village. There was nothing
more he wished to see here. With some difficulty, he once
more negotiated the narrow space between the gatepost and
the tree, and he was soon striding back up the gradient, away
from Castlequinn. Behind him, the narrow valley rang with
shrill, insane laughter.

There was no one about the crone's roadside cottage as he
passed it. The door was tightly shut, and dirty curtains had
been drawn across the windows. A thin strand of smoke rose
from the chimney, but that was the only sign of life about the
place. Nevertheless, Redmond kept tightly to the other side of
the road until he was well past the hovel, only resuming his

confident stride when it had disappeared around a corner behind him. Soon he was back at the junction and, turning left, took the road to Ardnahannon. The memories of the decayed village, the peculiar hag and the weak-minded youngster were already starting to fade. His hand still stung a little, though.

✛

Ardnahannon was all that the gazetteer had promised – a quaint village centred around an elaborate and beautiful stone Celtic cross. It seemed a relatively busy place, too, and the people whom Redmond met there greeted him civilly enough. He paused at a joining of the roads, close to the cross, to eat his lunch and enjoy the rest of the day. Across the road was a small shop, run by a large and jolly-looking woman who greeted her customers in a loud, mannish voice that carried right across the road to where he sat. Redmond smiled to himself as he clearly heard her salute 'Mr O'Hagan' and 'Mrs Monaghan', and devoured his sandwiches. He was much hungrier than he had imagined – the hill air had given him an appetite – and he wolfed them down with relish.

A tall man emerged from the shop, clutching some purchases to his chest as he closed the door behind him. 'Cheerio now, Mr Finucane!' called the shop-lady as he departed.

Redmond froze, as a memory of the all-but-deserted village sprang unbidden into his mind. Finucane – the name of the farmer who owned the place and who had sealed it off. The day seemed suddenly chillier. Gathering his bits and pieces together, Redmond rose and resumed his walk.

He took the Barnesmore road along the upper shores of Lough Maul, passing through the village without stopping. By early evening he arrived back at Mrs O'Dwyer's, footsore but refreshed.

'Did you have a good day, Mr Redmond?' she called out from the bar as he made his way up the back stairs to his room.

'Good enough!' he called back, trying to sound as cheery as he could. His hand was stinging a little more. Maybe Mrs O'Dwyer would have some disinfectant that he could dab on it. He would ask her at dinner – but if she hadn't, it was no great matter. The pain was irritating but not unbearable.

The walk to Ardnahannon had tired him more than he'd thought. Yawning, he washed himself in the narrow sink in the corner of his room and then sat down beside the window, which looked out over the roofs to the fields beyond. He had intended to read his gazetteer and plan something for the following day, but tiredness overcame him and he felt his head nodding forward on his chest in a delicious slumber.

Suddenly he was no longer in his warm room, seated in a comfortable armchair in the evening sunshine; he was sitting on a half-broken seat in the shadow-filled cottage back in Castlequinn. The place, however, was slightly different from the one he had visited earlier that day. It was still dark and cold, but there was a roaring fire burning in the fireplace (though it seemed to give out no heat at all), and the gloom was partly alleviated by this fire and by a single candle burning on the wooden mantelpiece. The chair on which Redmond sat seemed slightly sturdier than the wrecked skeleton he had seen in the falling cottage.

He shifted position slightly and found that he was not alone in the place. The shadow or discoloration on the stonework beside the chimney-breast was more substantial now, and it seemed to be moving of its own accord with a chilling, fluid motion. Redmond made to push it away and found that he could not; he could only move to a limited degree. The shadow, however, appeared to have no such restrictions: strengthened by the candlelight, it seemed to lean forward towards him, a nebulous arm stretched out in front of it. As Redmond tried to shrink back from it, the shadow seemed to touch him, and he felt a stinging pain in the palm of his hand. Somewhere in the distance, he thought he heard a voice, although it seemed to come from very far away: 'Ha! You devil! Ho! You devil! Foley! You devil!' coupled with a titter of insane laughter.

The fire blazed very brightly, strengthening the outlines of the shadow beside it, and the air around him seemed filled with mutterings and whisperings. Redmond pulled back – and woke with a start, bathed in sweat.

The final dregs of evening sun were falling through the window, and the room around him seemed perfectly in order. It had all been some sort of terrible dream!

And yet his hand still stung sharply. It was a nagging, jagged pain, like a bee-sting or an insect bite, and he instinctively rubbed at the palm, trying to ease it. His hand was wet and, looking down, he saw that the tiny wound had started to ooze blood again – no more than several pinprick-like drops, but enough to wet the centre of the palm. And, as he paused, the last of the muttering and whispering that he had heard in the nightmare seemed to die away around him in this very room. He waited as it fell to silence.

Rising from the chair, he went to the sink and ran his hand under the tap. When it was clean, he examined the wound. There were two little punctures on the skin, with a raised area around each, just as if he had been stung by an insect. Maybe, he thought in horror, the wound was infected and he should get it seen to. But his own doctor was back in England and he didn't know any medical practitioner in this area. Perhaps all it required was some disinfectant; Mrs O'Dwyer could see to that.

True to form, the landlady fussed over the injury. Redmond thought better of telling her how he had come by it.

'It's only a scratch!' he insisted. 'I think I got it climbing over a stone wall.' Given her earlier aversion to him visiting Castlequinn, he thought that the lie was probably worth it.

'It looks more like an insect bite, Mr Redmond,' she replied, squinting as she dabbed at it with a piece of cloth that she had dipped in iodine. 'Or the nip of a wee animal. Maybe you should get it seen to by a doctor.'

'There was probably something hiding among the stones of the wall when I jumped over it,' he lied. 'It might have given me a nip. But it's nothing. A drop of the "rare stuff" in your husband's pub'll soon set me up and make me forget about it.' And he gave a bit of a laugh.

Mrs O'Dwyer returned his humour with a wan and relatively mirthless smile, and he wondered if she knew how he had really come by the injury. There was something in her manner that suggested she might guess.

'I suppose it will, Mr Redmond,' she answered dryly. 'There now. All done!' And she wiped the cloth over the tiny wound with some finality. 'You'll be staying in for dinner tonight?'

He nodded. 'And then I can plan my walk for tomorrow,' he answered.

Again the dry smile. 'It might be best to stay close to the house tomorrow,' she said, almost knowingly. 'It's not going to be a good day.'

The pub was nearly empty; but then, it usually was. Redmond sat in the corner with a pint of Guinness and his maps on the table in front of him. From time to time, he rubbed his right hand against the leg of his trousers. It still pained him a little as the iodine stung at the wound. Behind the bar, Paddy O'Dwyer read the afternoon paper and spoke a few scant words to a couple of farmers at the other end of the bar, who were his only other customers.

Paddy, Redmond knew, was a fairly jolly man, full of chat, but sometimes subject to moods and fancies. Still, they got on well enough, and Paddy was certainly a storehouse of knowledge about the locality.

'Planning another trip up to see the hillbillies, Mr Redmond?' he called over with a laugh as he polished a glass.

Redmond looked up with a smile. 'I suppose so, Paddy,' he said, getting up and crossing to the counter. 'Maybe up as far as the old rath at Kildeeragh. Could you give me a Powers, please?' Paddy nodded and lifted down a whiskey glass. 'Is there much to see up there?'

Paddy opened the bottle. 'Oh, indeed there is, but you should be asking the wife, not myself. She's a Kildeeragh woman. A great rath, there is – covers the entire top of Kildeeragh Hill. There's an old, old church built inside of it – St Senlan's, they call it, I think – and a little graveyard. That's how big it is. Of course, the church is very small, and it's in ruins now, but it's still there.' He pushed the whiskey across the counter and took Redmond's money. 'Aye, I've heard the wife say that it used to be a very pagan place, and that there's a well somewhere up there in which they used to drown a child at the start of each year to ensure good luck.' Redmond winced visibly. 'But that was in the oul' pagan times, long ago. The wife would be able to tell you about all that.' Paddy gave a laugh and changed the subject. 'Have you travelled far today?'

'Ardnahannon.' Redmond lifted the glass and took a sip. The alcohol stung against his gums and he felt his palm jag him in sympathy. 'Over to Barnesmore, around Lough Maul.'

Paddy nodded. 'Ah, you can get a good view of the Lough up on Kildeeragh. You'll have seen the old Culdee cross at Ardnahannon Turn, then? Beautiful old thing, it is. And with a great history to it, I'm told. Did you come by the hills, then, Mr Redmond – over into Barnesmore?'

'Yes, indeed,' Redmond replied. His brow furrowed. 'Tell me, Paddy, did you ever hear of a farmer named Finucane who owns land in the Ardnahannon area?' It was a long shot, but he thought he'd try it – Paddy seemed to be more talkative than his wife. All the same, the landlord frowned.

'Ah, there's a number of Finucanes in that part of the world,' he said guardedly. 'There's Stephen Finucane, that lives by

the north side of Lough Maul and farms over between
Barnesmore and Sheely; there's Sean Finucane, that has land
around Ardnahannon Turn –'

'I was thinking of more towards Drumechtry and Roughfort,' Redmond prompted him.

The landlord seemed to think for a moment. 'There's a
Michael Finucane,' he said warily. 'Has land around the old
village at Castlequinn. But you wouldn't want to know
anything about him – now would he, Tony?' he shouted to
one of the farmers at the other end of the bar. The man turned
his head for a moment. 'Michael Finucane, out by Castlequinn?
You wouldn't want to know anything about him?' The man
gave a nervous laugh, waved a hand in the air and shook his
head. 'A sad, dark man, Mr Redmond. Tony there knows him,
and he would drink in here sometimes. Why do you ask?'

Redmond had to think quickly. 'An old woman that I met
on the road today,' he replied. 'Her name was …' He struggled
to remember the hag's name, but he couldn't. His hand was
stinging very badly now and he rubbed it against his side. 'No
matter. She mentioned the name to me. Said that he'd all the
lands round about closed off.'

Paddy took down another glass and wiped it slowly. 'That'd
be Michael Finucane, all right,' he answered. 'A dark, lonely
man if ever there was one. Had six of a family – all boys – and
every one not quite right in the head.' He shook his head sadly.
'Aye, he drinks in here sometimes, all right – but not that
often. The woman you met would've been his sister, Annie
Sullivan.'

Redmond recognised the name. He stared, aghast.

'His *sister*?' he exclaimed.

Paddy gave a half-smile. 'Oh, they haven't spoken in years,
Mr Redmond. In fact, I'm told that he charges her rent for the
bit of a cottage that she has. She's lived there ever since her
husband, old Seamus, died – he was a black oul' bugger, to be
sure – and her brother charges her rent for the place. Even

though she's his own sister. They hate each other, you see – it's the same with all Michael Finucane's family, they never had any luck. Not even his father, old Thomas. Not since .... '
He paused, as if he was going to say something more, but thought better of it.

'Annie Sullivan mentioned somebody else – said I was to ask about him. Somebody called Foley. She said that, if I ever met Michael Finucane, I was to ask about Foley. Do you know him as well, Paddy?'

The question was an innocent one, but it made Paddy O'Dwyer stop in his tracks. In the poor half-light of the bar, he seemed to have gone a little pale. All the same, he considered the question, his brow creasing. Redmond also noticed that the mere mention of the name had made the two farmers at the far end of the bar stop their conversation and look in his direction.

'Foley?' murmured Paddy. 'Foley? Can't say I know the name. You must remember, Mr Redmond, that oul' Annie's often wanderin' in her mind and sometimes pulls names out of nowhere. No, I know of no Foley round Castlequinn. You might ask the wife again, sir; she knows a lot more about that part of the world than I do. She might know a Foley.' And yet there was something in his manner that suggested to Redmond that he might be lying.

He shrugged and sipped at his whiskey. 'No matter!' he replied amiably. 'I was just curious. Old Annie Sullivan seemed so sure....' He thought it better not to mention the strange boy in the ruined village.

Paddy seemed to relax. 'Wanderin' in the mind, Mr Redmond. You're better takin' no notice of an oul' woman like that,' he said, almost condescendingly. 'They can tell you all sorts of foolish things. She's always been bitter against her brother, and this can make her mind not quite right, if you understand me. Pay her no heed at all, sir.' And he quickly changed the subject to some other topic.

Later, more farmers came in and the place became more lively. Even so, Redmond didn't completely join in the laughter and conversation – even though he had intended to do so. He felt peaky and somehow ill at ease, and he fancied an early night. Besides, his hand still hurt a little.

He had assumed he might have another nightmare that night, but his sleep was deep and dark and if he dreamed at all, they were disjointed, scattered dreams about trivial things. Even so, he was conscious of a dull ache in the palm of his hand that seemed to penetrate even his deepest slumber.

The next day he set off on another walk. It was what he had come to Galway for, and the weather was so good that he couldn't afford to waste a day of it. All the same, he was exhausted by the steep climb up to Kildeeragh. The view from the top of the hill, however, was worth it. The countryside lay spread out below him as far as the eye could see, and the calm waters of Lough Maul looked like a mirror, reflecting the near-cloudless sky.

The rath on the hill had been a large one, but most of it had been demolished long ago in order to make way for a small, now roofless church and an attendant graveyard. Apart from the view, there was really little to see, except for a few old walls (all that remained of the church), part of the dirt bank of the rath, and the small graveyard enclosed by a low stone wall, still intact, where long-headed weeds grew. Mrs O'Dwyer had told Redmond that St Senlan's had once been a burying-ground for certain families from the area around Ardnahannon, and their markers were still to be seen there – Malleys, McGillevreys, O'Dwyers. Some of her own ancestors slept in that peaceful spot, she had told him. He had said that he would have a look for them, but he hadn't asked her about Michael Finucane or Annie Sullivan. He had thought better of it. Besides, he was a little in awe of his landlady, for he'd heard that she could sometimes be as moody as her husband, and she mightn't take well to his questioning.

He didn't enter St Senlan's graveyard at first; he contented himself with admiring the view from all sides of the hill. It was as he passed behind the little church that he noticed something odd. Just outside the enclosure, a single worn tombstone rose out of the tall grasses. In fact, it was so well concealed amongst the weeds and low bushes that he might have missed it completely. It was certainly not part of the overall cemetery; it stood a little way back from the wall, as if to create some distance between its incumbent and those who slept within the church grounds.

The single stone drew Redmond to it, and he bent down to read its inscription. The winds at the top of Kildeeragh had done their work, and the marker was badly weathered; even so, some words were still faintly legible. Squatting down beside the stone, he pushed away the trailing grasses and squinted at the inscription. In the harsh, brassy light of the early-afternoon sun, he made out the tracks of words, following them with his fingers to be sure what they said. Some of the inscription was gone, but the part he could make out puzzled him. As far as he could follow it, the legend ran: '… EL …' (Daniel? Samuel? Michael? The stone was so worn that the rest of the name was gone.) '… LENNOX FOLEY 187….' The rest of the date was indecipherable.

Redmond stiffened slightly as he recognised the name Annie Sullivan had mentioned. There was something else – no more than a couple of lines – but he couldn't follow the letters over the wind-smoothed stone. However, the final words, which had been placed near the bottom of the marker, had been incised so deeply that they were still legible. His fingers traced the letters. 'IN THE NAME OF GOD BE STILL.' That was all.

His brow furrowing in puzzlement, Redmond straightened up. This was a mystery, all right! Who was this Samuel, Michael or Daniel Lennox Foley, and why had he been buried outside the church wall at St Senlan's? And what was the meaning of the queer phrase, 'In the name of God be still'?

He looked at the stone again, trying to squeeze the last drop of information from it. He thought he could make out a word that began with a capital 'CA' and ended in 'INN'. Could it be 'Castlequinn'? he wondered. The word certainly seemed to be the right length. He looked more closely, but he couldn't be sure – the lettering was so worn. Still wondering, he made a cursory exploration of the church and graveyard – as he had surmised, there was little to see in the ruin, and those headstones that he could read simply bore names and dates of local people – before turning back down Kildeeragh Hill towards the lowlands.

Questions concerning the overgrown tombstone bothered Redmond all the way back to the pub. The bar was full when he arrived there, and he could have called in for a drink, but he thought he'd go straight to his room and lie down. He was feeling very tired, perhaps from the walk, which seemed to have taken longer than he'd imagined; and, besides, his hand was starting to hurt again.

He lay down on the bed but couldn't settle. The pain in his palm had turned to a dull, nagging ache that wouldn't let him even doze off. Besides, his head was buzzing with more and more queries. Just who was Foley? Why had he been buried outside the wall at St Senlan's? Was he a suicide, or an unbaptised child maybe (Redmond had no dates for the unknown's lifespan)? Part of the name on the stone had been 'Lennox' – was this related to the Adam Lennox whom the gazetteer had mentioned, the strange Norman churchman who had once inhabited the old castle? What was the meaning of the strange inscription – 'In the name of God be still'? Why had Paddy O'Dwyer avoided mentioning Foley? Redmond was sure that the landlord had known about him. What was his connection to the mysterious Michael Finucane? Why had Annie Sullivan asked Redmond to mention him to the reclusive farmer if they should ever meet?

He tossed on the bed as more and more questions poured through his raging mind. At last he could rest no longer; he went over to the washstand to splash his face and hands with water, in preparation for going downstairs to have a meal. In front of the stand a mirror hung, and Redmond was able to see himself as he threw the water against his skin, feeling its coldness sting him slightly. He looked again.

His wet face was still there in the foreground, as were his shoulders, wearing the same checked shirt; but the scene behind him had changed dramatically. Once again, he was looking into the interior of the cottage in Castlequinn. Once again he saw the dirty stone wall behind him, with its narrow window spilling vague shards of light across the flagstone floor; and, to his left, there was the interior door leading off into another part of the cottage. On it was the faint reflection of a burning fire, and he had the impression that the mirror had been placed on the mantelpiece so that it reflected most of the room.

And to his left the shadow, or whatever it was, was moving towards him. He sensed it, even though he could not actually see it in the glass, for there was a suggestion of movement close by – as if someone or something were reaching out to touch him. Added to that, the air around him was suddenly full of mutterings and whisperings, as if people were talking far away. He shook his head to try and clear the sensation, but it wouldn't go away. He felt the wound on his hand sting again, and a roaring blackness seemed to spring from the mirror to envelop him....

The bedroom was suddenly back again, and everything steadied around him. Redmond gripped the edge of the washstand and looked into the mirror. All he could see was the familiar bed, the crumpled sheet where he'd been lying, and some maps spread out on a nearby table. Everything was solid, familiar and homely. His hand, however, was still dully painful, and, looking down, he saw a thin trickle of blood running down on the white porcelain. The sounds in the air seemed to fade, although he still thought he heard a voice far away – a voice that cried 'Foley!' and coupled it with a titter of laughter before it too faded.

The wound on his palm was bleeding again. Wrapping a towel around it, he made his way over to a seat by the window and almost fell into it as the vision gradually subsided. When his strength had fully returned, he went to his case, took out a box of sticking-plasters and applied one to the wound on his palm. Slowly he began to feel better, even hungry. Leaving the room as it was, he went down to get something to eat.

The small crowd was still in the bar after dinner. A fiddle player had taken up residence in a corner by the open fire and was rendering a lively air that had some farmers by the counter clapping their hands in time to the music. Wending his way amongst them, Redmond sought out his usual seat and ordered a pint of stout from Paddy, who was his usual cheerful self.

'Good day, Mr Redmond?' he asked as Redmond took his first draught. Redmond nodded, still drawing off the creamy head. 'And where were you today? Kildeeragh, was it?'

'I was,' answered Redmond. 'Up at the old rath and the old church.'

Paddy smiled. 'St Senlan's? Oldest church in these parts. I've heard the wife say that it's one of the oldest in Ireland. There's families lying up in Kildeeragh from well before the Famine. You'll find most of the old families there, all right!' He lowered his voice slightly. 'Look over to the other end of the bar, just by the door. There's a man you were askin' about standing against the wall – the man with the queer-lookin' boy. That's Michael Finucane.'

Redmond cast a glance at the tall, dark, sour-looking man who was sipping his pint in the corner. His gaze wandered to the young man at his side, and he froze. It was the same person he'd seen at Castlequinn! And, as he watched, the boy turned his head and looked towards him with a blank, empty gaze, not recognising him at all. Suddenly the air seemed momentarily filled with the familiar whisperings and mutterings; but in an instant that was gone, and the reassuring sounds of the barroom were back.

'Is that –' He choked out the words; they would barely come. 'Is that his son with him?'

Paddy O'Dwyer squinted. 'Oh, yes, that's Michael Óg, his eldest. He's the queerest of the whole bunch. Goes wandering off into the hills over by Castlequinn and is never seen for days. They say he lives in the abandoned houses there. They say he talks to the fairies.' He gave a throaty chuckle and went to serve another customer.

Looking across the bar, Redmond noted that the boy had never lifted his blank eyes from him. It was as if Michael Óg was trying to remember who he might be. The effect was utterly unnerving. Quickly, Redmond left by a side door and hurried back to his room.

Throwing himself into a chair, he wiped away the sweat that was already starting to bead around his brow. His hand felt wet, and he saw that blood had oozed out from under the plaster, along the edges of his palm. He washed it under the tap and applied a new sticking-plaster, then lay down on the bed and sank into a deep and troubled sleep.

This time he did dream – a clear and horrifying nightmare, which he seemed to be watching as if from a distance. It was like watching a film. He stood in the low hall of a castle; it stretched away in front of him to a large fire at the far end. In front of the blaze, an old man stretched out a hand for warmth. The fire flared up and burned brightly, casting huge and monstrous shadows against the stone walls all around. The hall was a plain place with dull stonework, hung with a couple of pennants but little more. The old man himself was dressed in drab colours, browns and blacks, the clothes of a previous era – maybe, thought Redmond, the attire of the mid-sixteenth century – and he leaned heavily on a large stick. He appeared to be blind.

Around him, shadows wheeled and moved against the stonework of the chimney-breast, and amongst these shadows Redmond thought he detected a furtive movement. Men were creeping up on the old man, out of the darkness. A knife-blade glinted in the firelight. Redmond opened his mouth to shout a warning, but no sound would come.

Even so, the old man turned from the blaze, and for the first time Redmond saw his face. In the ruddy glow of the firelight, the skin seemed as grey and drab as the antique clothing, but it also appeared heavily lined and slightly twisted with age. These lines gave it an almost predatory look, like that of a vulpine beast about to pounce. A large, hooked nose added to the feral image, and the tangles of a long, greying beard all but concealed a cruel, lopsided mouth. In all his life, Redmond had never seen such evil written large on a human countenance. Its sinister aspect was accentuated by the two great eyes, white with cataracts, which seemed to survey the hall around them.

The old man spoke – doubtless asking if there was anyone close by – but Redmond heard nothing. In the shadows, an arm was raised and the knife flashed again in the fire's glow. Sensing danger, the blind man threw up his hands – but too late. Men stepped from the darkness around the fire, holding swords and daggers. Blow upon blow rained on the blind man's shoulders. He slumped forward, and the flagstones on the floor of the hall ran red with spilling blood. Only then did Redmond hear the shrill scream of the dying blind man.

By now he could see at least some of the assailants' faces in the firelight. Chief amongst them was a tall, grim man, dressed in dark sixteenth-century clothes, who shared many of the facial characteristics of the blind man at his feet – the hooked nose, the twisted, scowling lip. Dark, greasy hair hung below his collar, and a great, vivid scar ran from the left-hand corner of his brow to the edge of his lip, cutting across a gouged-out eye in the process. He aimed a kick at the fallen blind man. Behind him, other ruffians stepped into the firelight, swords at the ready. The obviously dying man raised a hand, desperately trying to rise, but the scarred murderer spat at him and he sank to the flagstones once again.

One of the other ruffians suddenly gripped his leader's arm and pointed at a shadowy stretch of wall beside the great fireplace. In his dream, Redmond strained to see but could make out nothing but darkness and shadows. However, he heard the brigand utter one word – 'Lennox!'

He moved a little closer, the dream making the motion seem slow and awkward, like walking through treacle. The section of the wall to which the murderer pointed was slightly darker than the stonework around it and appeared to be growing darker by the second. Blurred edges were suddenly becoming clearer, shaping themselves into the outline of a human shadow.

The brigands drew back, and even their black-haired leader crossed himself as if against some awful evil. Then, as if somehow aware of Redmond's presence, he slowly turned his head, the firelight catching the socket of his missing eye....

Redmond woke with a start, his palm aching. Looking at his watch, he realised that he'd been asleep for no more than a couple of hours, although it felt much longer. As the dream slowly faded and reality reasserted itself, he began to try to make some sense of the striking nightmare. He had no doubt that he had somehow witnessed the murder of Tadgh Dall O'Choinn by his half-brother Fergananam at Castlequinn, many centuries earlier. He also believed that it had something to do with his own visit to the ruined village, and with the wound on his hand.

He rose from the bed and staggered to the mirror; the room behind him remained the same. Splashing his face with water, he saw that the wound on his palm was oozing blood again – not as much as before, but enough to give a faint crimson tinge to the tap-water. The edges of the plaster he'd put across it had come away, allowing a trickle to seep out.

He applied a fresh piece to it; and as he did so, he became aware of a commotion drifting up from the bar below him. Voices were raised, and there seemed to be somebody shouting over the general hubbub. Opening his door, Redmond went to the top of the stairs to listen. A familiar voice was shouting across the bar, and Redmond strained forward a little to hear what was said.

'Foley! You devil! I know you're here. Ha! Spawn of Black Lennox! Ha! You devil!' It was the voice of the weak-minded boy from Castlequinn. There was a faint commotion and a man's low voice, obviously trying to placate the speaker. 'Foley's here!' the voice persisted. 'He's here, come from his place by the fire in Castlequinn. Come out, you devil!'

Creeping down the stairs, Redmond peered around the corner of a door; from there, he could see the bar. Michael Finucane was ushering his son out of the place as heads turned to see him go. 'Spawn of Black Lennox!' the boy was shouting. 'He's here! In this place! He's come from his place by the fire! Come out, you devil!'

With a few low words that Redmond couldn't hear, Michael Finucane pushed his son through the main doors, pulling them closed behind him. The bar returned to its normal drone. Seeing Redmond looking round the corner of the door, Paddy O'Dwyer smiled and shook his head, but said nothing.

Redmond returned to his room and went to bed. He slept fitfully all night.

✟

'I've something here for you, Mr Redmond,' Mrs O'Dwyer called to him next morning as he came down to breakfast. 'It's just a little thing that I thought might be of some use to you.' And she thrust a small booklet into his hand. 'It's a book on local history that belonged to my uncle. It's been lying about the house, and I thought you could make some use of it.' The booklet was old, yellowed and crumbling, with some of its pages threatening to fall out. 'It'll give you a background to your ramblings round the country,' she added with a smile.

Redmond thanked her, promised to look at it and went on to breakfast. His hand was hurting badly, although it seemed to have stopped oozing blood.

Later, in his room, he examined the booklet. He felt too tired to go walking through the hills, as he'd planned; he thought that a more restful day – pottering about the immediate locality, coupled with a little bit of reading – might be more in order. Besides, he was worried that the stress that had originally brought him down here was starting to reassert itself. Rest and relaxation were what he needed, without the added strain of going hiking over hillside roads.

Sitting down in his customary seat by the window, he turned the pages of the booklet. Some of them were yellowed to the point of being brown, and their edges had a flaky quality to them. The pamphlet was clearly very old, and when Redmond turned to the title page, he found that it had been printed in 1891. Its contents were rather uninteresting – just a vague, generalised guide to the history of the area. His gazetteer actually gave him more information. However, one entry did catch his eye.

The village of Castlequinn is now only sparsely inhabited. A minor castle once stood there, but now only a few stones remain. Reputedly built in the twelfth century, this fortress was once the stronghold of Adam Lennox, a religious eccentric who was widely believed to be a warlock. During the sixteenth century it was occupied by a sept of the O'Choinns or O'Quinns, who gave the area its name. Most of the edifice has since been demolished and the stones used for building purposes within

the surrounding village. It is thought that during
Famine times a number of the nearby cottages were
built with dressed stone from this castle.

Redmond turned the fragile page to find that that was all there
was. Setting the books aside, he was starting to rise when the
scene around him suddenly changed once more. The
comfortable walls of the bedroom faded away, to be replaced
by the dank stonework of the ruined cottage at Castlequinn.
This time, he was facing a blazing fire, burning in the hearth;
beside it, the discoloration or shadow or whatever it was moved
and writhed as if to welcome him. Like a sleepwalker, he
involuntarily moved forward towards it, his hand outstretched.
He felt the cold roughness of the wall against his skin and
another insect-like prick into his flesh. Mutterings filled the
damp and unhealthy air around him, whispers of voices only
half-heard.

The impression was only momentary, and as Redmond
blinked with the pain of the tiny bite, the vision faded and he
was back in his bedroom again. Looking down at his palm, he
saw that the sticking-plaster had been torn away and that the
wound was bleeding profusely. Several drops of blood fell
messily to the floor, and one splashed on his shoe.

Rushing to the washstand, he staunched the bleeding with
some paper towels, which he wound round his hand as a
makeshift bandage. The muttering in his head receded, but he
still felt dizzy and slightly nauseated. What was happening to
him? Was he on the verge of nervous collapse once more?

He would have to seek medical help, he decided, not only
for his continually bleeding hand but also to settle his mind
and stabilise himself again. There was a doctor not far away;
he would ask Mrs O'Dwyer about him or her. Once more he
lay down on his bed, feeling the room spin around him, and
stayed there until the bleeding stopped and he was able to
throw the reddened towels in the bin and cover the scratches
with yet more plasters.

Mrs O'Dwyer told him that Dr Kennedy was a fine man –
for a Protestant. He had been the district doctor for more years
than she could remember, and he'd personally brought at least
three of her own brood of six into the world.

'He'll see you without an appointment, Mr Redmond,' she
told him. 'Just go up to the house beyond the filling station
and see Mrs O'Boyle, his receptionist. It's as well to get that
cut looked at. I think you might have got an infection in it.'

She was right about the doctor's availability, at least. Dr
Kennedy saw Redmond almost at once – indeed, he appeared
to be the doctor's only patient. Kennedy was an elderly man,
tall and smelling slightly of cigarette smoke, with greying
temples and overly thick glasses from behind which hazel eyes
squinted warily. He listened as Redmond told him about the
scratch on his palm and about feeling 'stressed' in the bedroom
– he didn't mention the visions.

'You should get in contact with your own doctor as soon
as you go back home,' Dr Kennedy advised, reaching out to
take Redmond's hand and inspect the wound. 'You said you're
here for only a few more days? I'd make the appointment now
and see him as soon as you get back.' He looked at the scratch.
'In fact, I would … Good God!' His lined face paled a little,
and his body seemed to stiffen. 'Where did you get this – ah –
scratch? Jumping over a wall, you said?'

Redmond nodded. 'A dry stone wall. It's some sort of bite
from a tiny animal among the stones, isn't it?' he offered lamely.

The doctor looked up, staring directly into his face. 'Have
you been anywhere near Castlequinn?' he enquired, his voice
heavy with meaning. 'In all my years of practice, I've only
seen two of these before, and they were both associated with
that damn place.'

Redmond nodded, feeling his face reddening at the lie he'd
told the doctor. 'I've been there,' he admitted. 'And it's where
I got the scratch. From an old wall inside one of the houses
there.' Was it his imagination, or did Dr Kennedy blanch even

further? Certainly his eyes widened behind his thick glasses.

'You've been *inside* the houses?' he asked. Then, getting up, he crossed to the door. 'Mrs O'Boyle,' he called, 'put on some tea and bring us both in a cup. And if anyone else calls, tell them I might be a wee while.'

'What is it?' Redmond was becoming alarmed.

Dr Kennedy sat down again. He seemed to think for a moment.

'Can I ask if you've been experiencing nightmares of any sort? Even when you think you're awake?' he asked.

Redmond froze.

'How – how did you know? That's what I meant when I said that I was stressed. They're almost like ... religious visions.'

Kennedy snorted. 'They're anything but religious. I assume they're concerned with Castlequinn itself?' Redmond looked wonderingly at him. 'You're not the first to be plagued with them. I've heard of them before; so did my father and grand-father –' The door opened, and Mrs O'Boyle brought in a pot of tea and two cups.

'I already had the kettle on,' she explained. Kennedy thanked her and she left, shooting Redmond a queer look over her shoulder.

Dr Kennedy poured the tea, then, lifting his cup, sat back.

'Four generations of Kennedys have been doctors in this district,' he began. 'My great-grandfather was a doctor here just after the Famine. I'll probably be the last of the line. Both my father and my grandfather had a great interest in local history, and both actually wrote pamphlets on the subject – I have only a passing interest.' He took another sip of tea, and Redmond did likewise. 'Even though my family is Protestant and most of the community here is Catholic, we have always enjoyed the confidence of our patients, and we've heard plenty of things that wouldn't be talked about anywhere else. So what I'm about to tell you must remain in absolute confidence between us. Do I have your word on that?' He replaced his cup on the edge of the table, and Redmond noticed that his hand was shaking.

'You have my word,' Redmond replied.

Kennedy sat further back in his chair.

'Just after I joined the practice as a junior doctor, my father, who was the senior partner, brought me in to look at a case. An old man had come in with a peculiar bite on his arm. At first I thought it was the nip of a very small animal, but the man had lost so much blood that I couldn't be sure. The man was a farmer who held lands over by Castlequinn. His name was Thomas Finucane – his son Michael still farms there – and he was a stubborn, twisted old man. But when I saw him, he was very badly shaken.'

Dr Kennedy licked his lips and continued. 'The remains of the village were on his lands, and he planned to pull the old houses down and use the land for grazing. There was a superstition about the place, but he paid it no heed. He had gone through what remained of the village to see if he could use what stonework was left. In one of the houses, something had bitten him. Does that sound familiar?'

Redmond made no response. The horror of the doctor's story was sending a coldness along his back.

'And do you know what he said had bitten him? A shadow. He said he'd seen some sort of darkness on the wall beside the fireplace in one of the cottages – Foley's old cottage, he said it was ...' Redmond felt a thrill pass through him at the mention of the name. '... and something had bitten him. At first he'd thought there was something in the wall, but then he'd imagined that it was the shadow itself. Shortly afterwards, he'd started to experience some sort of dream each night.'

Kennedy lifted the cup to his lips again. As he sipped the tea, the colour seemed to be steadily draining from his face. 'He always dreamed that he was back in the cottage and that the shadow was trying to bite him again. His wife was dead and he slept alone, but he always woke up to find his bedclothes

soaked in blood from his arm. At first he'd bandaged the arm
up and gone on about his business, but then the dreams – or
whatever they were – started tormenting him in the daytime
as well. He'd be sitting down after his dinner and he'd suddenly
imagine himself back in that cottage again, over in Castlequinn,
with a great fire roaring in the hearth and the shadow reaching
out from the stonework beside the fireplace. He would always
wake up to find his arm bleeding, as if he'd somehow cut it.

'I could see that Father was extremely worried, and I was
vastly surprised when he told me that there was nothing he
could do. He advised Finucane to go and see the priest. I don't
know if he did that or not. Shortly afterwards, though, I heard
that Thomas Finucane was dead. He was a twisted, bitter old
man and was barely missed from the community.' Kennedy
paused again and looked out of the window, across the hills. 'I
challenged Father, of course, and he told me a queer story that
he'd heard from his grandfather – my great-grandfather.'

'You mentioned a name there,' Redmond reminded him,
'Foley. I've seen it on a tombstone up at Kildeeragh, and I
heard a strange boy running about the ruins at Castlequinn,
shouting it....'

Dr Kennedy smiled. 'Ah, yes! Michael Óg, Michael
Finucane's son.'

'There was an old woman – Annie Sullivan – who told me
to mention it if I ever met Michael Finucane. Does my – ah –
sickness have something to do with this Foley person?'

Dr Kennedy leaned forward.

'Indeed it does. Dark Annie was right – many in this district
say that Gabriel Foley was the root of all the evil that befell
Castlequinn. Do you fancy something stronger?' He nodded
towards a nearby cabinet. Redmond didn't refuse as the doctor
brought out a bottle of whiskey and two glasses.

'My great-grandfather knew Gabriel Foley, for Foley was
alive when he was doctor here. Foley was a peculiar old man
who was almost a clan patriarch in the village. They said that

he could trace his lineage back to the O'Quinns who held the lands in the sixteenth century – aye, and even further back.' He held out a glass of whiskey to Redmond, who accepted it readily.

'You might have heard of Adam Lennox, who is supposed to have held the old castle at Castlequinn during the twelfth century. Although he was a monk of some kind, legend says that he was also a warlock and that he raised the Devil in the castle grounds. If you believe these old stories, then you'll believe that the Devil granted him a kind of immortality, and that the black soul of the warlock was somehow fused with the very stones of the castle itself – particularly the area beside the fireplace in the great hall, where Lennox used to sit. There's a belief in this part of the world, you see, that great evil can imbue inanimate objects such as wood and stone. So the discoloration in the wall was also strengthened by the murder of Blind Tadhg O'Quinn in the 1500s. He was rumoured to be a warlock and a drinker of blood – particularly the blood of those whom he slew in battle.

'Anyway, Gabriel Foley claimed to be descended from Black Lennox as well, and there were rumours that Foley himself was a magician. The folk around Castlequinn didn't dare to cross him. When the castle of the O'Quinns was finally pulled down, just before the Famine, Gabriel claimed some of the old stones – including the fireplace from the hall – to make repairs to his own house. He took the discoloured piece of wall and placed it in his cottage, next to his fireplace. Of course, this strengthened the rumours about him being a sorcerer, but he didn't seem to care. People said that, each time they called to see him, the discoloration had grown stronger and darker. Foley himself seemed to be fading away; but, although my great-grandfather knew about his condition, the old man never asked him to call.

'Then the Famine hit the village, and hit it very hard. Although he appeared weak, Gabriel Foley organised the villagers; he may well have saved some of their lives. He got them to drink blood – cows' blood. Oh, that was common enough in some parts of Clare and Galway, but Foley appears to have turned it into an art form amongst the villagers of Castlequinn. Scores of Finucane cattle – most of their herd – were used for blood-letting in the village street. A vein in the neck would be opened, and the villagers would drink the warm blood that gushed out. They mixed it with what oatmeal they had and with turnip-tops. Some of them, like Foley, drank it raw. In that way – a horrible way, but a lifesaver nonetheless – they kept themselves alive.

'It was said that Foley himself drank more than cows' blood – that he took blood from the dying in the farms about Ardnahannon. He would let himself into the houses at night and attack the old and feeble, drinking what blood he could from them, like a vampire. People whispered that the horror of the Famine had given him a taste for blood. That was what they said, but nobody could ever prove it, and people feared Foley too much to ever say it out loud. They still fear him....'

'You mean to say that he's still alive?' Redmond almost shouted incredulously, gripped by the sheer horror of it all.

The doctor took another sip from his cup. 'After a fashion,' he answered. 'There are people who believe that he might still be about. The Finucanes, of course: they complained about what was happening to their cattle, and Foley is supposed to have cursed them. They gave birth to feeble-minded boys – all Michael's brothers were either completely insane or a bit "touched", and all his sons are certainly weak mentally. The land will be sold once he dies. There are those who will tell you – and Dark Annie Sullivan, Michael's own sister, is one of them – that the Finucane line is blighted by Gabriel Foley's curse.

'I'm told that Foley lived at Castlequinn right up until the turn of this century – my grandfather remembered him still living there – and that he was one of the last to do so. After he was dead, the Finucanes shut up the village, sealing it off with barbed wire and makeshift hedges. Local people feared that he might come back; and, because he was thought to be a great warlock, he was buried outside the old cemetery at St Senlan's.'

'"In the name of God, be still,"' whispered Redmond softly, almost to himself.

'That was what they put on his gravestone,' agreed Kennedy. 'He was an evil man, true enough – my grandfather always said so.'

His eyes narrowed and he looked directly at Redmond. 'They say that he's still out there – or, at least, a part of him is. The discoloration on the wall, according to local superstition, is his essence, and the essence of Blind Tadhg, and the essence of Adam Lennox from all those centuries ago. It somehow became infused into the stone that was taken from the castle, and they say that it has a life of its own. That's why nobody'll talk about Gabriel Foley, nor even mention his name – in case the Thing in Castlequinn *knows*. And it's said that, if you touch it with your bare flesh, it can have power over you – the power to draw you to it whenever it wants to drink. Even though it's long dead, it can still draw sustenance from the living.

'Of course, as a medical man and as a man of the twentieth century, I'd have to tell you that it's nothing more than an old country superstition. But as a local man, and as a doctor who's seen too many queer things, I'd have to say that there might be something in the tale. Thomas Finucane wasn't the only one who's come to me with the same story about the village. And now there's you....'

'And the weak-minded son?' asked Redmond. 'I saw him wandering about in the old village. Is he infected too?'

Kennedy shook his head. 'Poor Michael Óg. Yes, he sometimes wanders about the village; I'm told he sleeps in the old houses. He believes that Foley is still there and shouts for him to come out, all to no avail. I'm told that Dark Annie

Sullivan sometimes goes down to the village too. Neither of
them seems to be affected by the shadow. Maybe it's because
they're both weak-minded.'

He shifted position in the seat. 'But, like my father, I really
think there's little that I, as a medical man, can do for you.
You need to see a priest or a minister. I've a feeling that the
thing is supernatural rather than natural; and, while I can
deal with afflictions that beset the body, I can't do anything
about things that beset the soul, other than to tell you all that
I know.' He rose. 'And, of course, I can pray for you. But you
should go and see your clergyman as quickly as possible.'

The door opened a little, and Mrs O'Boyle poked her head
around it.

'Doctor, Mr Egan's here for his appointment. He's been
waiting for ages and I didn't like to disturb you, but....'

Kennedy waved her apology away. 'It's all right. We're
just finished.' He gripped Redmond's shoulder. 'Please, do see
a clergyman. See what he can do for you. I beg you to see him
as quickly as you can. It's all beyond my powers – I'm sure
you understand....' There was something half-apologetic in his
tone.

Redmond nodded and followed Mrs O'Boyle out of the
surgery. Kennedy watched him go with a helpless expression
on his weathered face. Somehow, he looked even greyer.

✢

Out on the road again, walking back towards Mrs O'Dwyer's,
Redmond mulled over what the doctor had said. He had been
advised to seek out a priest or minister, but he was not a
particularly religious man. He believed, he had always told
himself, in the power of the mind, rather than in the power of
an invisible and unproven soul. The rational, scientific side of
his mind was gradually beginning to take over. What if Kennedy
was wrong? He was a local man, after all; what if he was

simply repeating – what had he called it? – 'an old country superstition'? What if, even though Kennedy denied it, his mind was mired with old traditions? Redmond found that he was gradually becoming tired of the gullibility of these people. If he were to accept what they said, then his own mind would go reeling back to the stress and terror that he had come here to escape.

No, the answer didn't lie with a priest or a minister – it probably lay back in Castlequinn itself. Kennedy had been wrong: there was some natural explanation for it all. Maybe the roughness of the ancient stonework had created the wound on his palm, while the discoloration on the cottage wall was no more than some sort of lichen, which had infected the cut in some way, making him experience weird visions. All that talk about Gabriel Foley was just so much nonsense. An old man who had been one of the last inhabitants of a crumbling village, who already had a reputation as a sorcerer amongst the credulous people round about – was it any wonder that stories had grown up about him?

And Kennedy might well have embellished the stories in order to connect them with the wound. No doubt he had hoped that Redmond would see his own doctor and take his problem somewhere else. That was probably the way of it in these parochial, inward-looking communities. Well, he *would* see his own doctor as soon as he got home; but, just in case the lichen in the cottage was some sort of hallucinogen, it might be well to have a sample of it to analyse.

That meant that he would have to go back to Castlequinn. Still, he had no fear of that place any more. What was it, anyway? Just a huddle of abandoned houses! It was still reasonably early in the day, and he could reach it by early afternoon. In that way, he would also confront the demons that had been tormenting him; he would face his own unease head-on.

With a newfound confidence, he strode along the road towards O'Dwyer's pub.

✦

Several hours' brisk walking took Redmond back to the fork in the upland road above Ardnahannon. To his left, the road sloped down the steep bank towards Castlequinn. Without hesitating this time, Redmond turned and strode towards the hidden village.

Rounding a bend, he came on Annie Sullivan's hovel, tucked into the side of the bank. There was no sign of life about it, although that same thin strand of smoke wafted from the chimney in the still afternoon air. With a sort of confident light-headedness, Redmond thought he might stop and tell her that he knew all about Foley. A few stern raps on the peeling door brought no response, although he sensed that she was there, watching him from behind the dirty curtains. He abandoned the attempt and continued on down the hill towards the village below.

This time, he eased himself through the gap in Finucane's barrier without too much trouble and was soon walking slowly up the overgrown street, between the falling cottages. The place didn't seem to be in quite such a state of deterioration as he had remembered it. Some of the houses, though roofless, were actually quite sturdy, and he could imagine that this might have been a rather pleasant community in some former time. From a fallen doorway, a wide-eyed sheep watched him as he passed.

Where the turf road swung to the right, up towards the plateau, the door to the low-roofed cottage lay open. Inside there was only gloom, but Redmond didn't hesitate; he strode into the dwelling.

It was as he remembered – the flagstoned floor, the sagging chair with its broken support, the yawning mouth of the fireplace, the closed door to another room, shadows and spiderwebs everywhere. From somewhere nearby, a crow cawed loudly and warningly.

There, beside the empty fireplace, was the eerie shape against the grey stonework. It seemed to have more definition about it, somehow; it had taken on a vaguely man-shaped form. And, as Redmond stepped forward, it seemed to writhe and move a little, as if in anticipation. He put it down to a trick of the feeble light trickling through the narrow windows.

'Now then!' he said, advancing towards the wall. 'Let's see what you're made of.' Once again he reached out and touched it.

There was the thrill of cold stone against his fingertips, a thrill that travelled along Redmond's arm like an electric shock. It was like suddenly dipping his hand into a dark, freezing pool. Then he gasped, taken aback, and his brain reeled as unbidden thoughts darted through his mind. He glimpsed the great hall of a castle, in flames, with men battling with swords in its centre; a face seemed superimposed on the scene – a narrow, evil face with long hanks of greasy hair and white cataracts over both eyes – the face of the man whom he had seen murdered in his dream. Then he stood in the centre of the cottage; outside the shapes of people moved, carrying what appeared to be bowls brimming with some viscous red substance. As if from far away, he heard the lowing of cattle. In front of him was a bowl of dark redness, and, to his horror, he felt himself lowering his face and drinking from it.

The cow-sounds changed, and he heard a harsh, thick voice – was it that of the crow he'd heard earlier? – calling out in heavy tones, chanting. Although he couldn't understand it, he recognised the language as a form of Latin. Instinctively, he knew that this was the sonorous voice of Adam Lennox, the man who had brought evil to this place by his witchcraft, shouting to him across the centuries. The air around him was suddenly thick with muttering. The sound seemed to flow from the stones all around, stones that had been brought from the polluted castle.

Redmond's confidence had suddenly left him, and he felt

inexplicably weak. Looking down, he saw that his hand was bleeding again. He staggered towards the falling chair, his bloody hand grasping at its back to steady himself. Disjointed images and impressions swarmed about him – fire, swords, faces, cottages, the interior of a castle, shadows – making his mind swim. He sank into the chair, which, miraculously, held his weight. In front of him, the man-shaped shadow began to expand; in his mind's eye, Redmond saw a fire burning in the grate and the discoloration spreading out across the surrounding stone like a dark stain. It seemed to reach for him.

'In the name of God, be still!' he murmured through almost-useless lips; but it was far too late. The musty blackness of the shadow swirled about him like a cloak, filling his ears with its senseless mutterings. Far away, the voice shouted again in the Latin-like tongue. Redmond sank back.

Later, when he didn't return to the pub, the O'Dwyers would inform the Gardaí, who would organise a hunt for him. His body, utterly drained of blood, would be found on the floor of the abandoned cottage in Castlequinn by Michael Finucane, looking for one of his animals. Blood would be staining the flagstones around him, and he be dead.

But now, as his consciousness slipped away from him forever, all he heard was another voice shouting, closer at hand. A young man's voice:

'Foley! Ha! You devil! Ho! You devil!'

THE WAY THROUGH
THE WOOD

Sinéad had always hated the wood – the way the sly trees seemed to come together as though whispering strange secrets to one another; the half-light, stealing between the branches, which always seemed to hide more than it showed; the way the paths twisted on each other as though deliberately trying to mislead anyone unfortunate enough to travel along them. She hated the suffocating closeness of the woodland foliage and the furtiveness of unseen animals as they scuttled amongst it.

The wood came down to the large field that lay just behind her Aunt Barbara's and Uncle Joe's house, where she had spent each childhood summer holiday. From the window of her bedroom, she could see the nodding trees, rising like a green and sinister curtain at the other side of the open expanse. From time to time, sheep or cattle grazing in the fields would stare back at her; it seemed that none of them wandered too close to the faraway tree-line. Nor had she gone there herself. Both her aunt and her uncle were fond of walking in the countryside; but the suggestion of crossing the field and going for a stroll in the deep woodlands.... It had seemed, even in those early days, that there was something about the wood that kept decent people, like her aunt and uncle, away from it.

Over twelve years ago, after Uncle Joe had his first heart attack, the summer holidays in County Longford had stopped. Aunt Barbara was 'getting on a bit', and now that her energies were concentrated on looking after a sick husband, she wasn't really able to cater for Sinéad. Besides, there was far more activity in Dublin. Sinéad's younger brother and sister were starting to grow up, and were taking more of an interest in going out; Sinéad herself had started going to youth clubs and had begun notice boys for the first time. Her aunt and uncle's house didn't seem to have the same appeal. Longford, she thought, was a strange county anyway – long empty roads, scattered houses, villages huddled away in the folds of the land, endless deserted fields – and now it held no attraction for her at all. She still dropped Aunt Barbara the occasional note, enquiring how Uncle Joe was and asking for any news from the countryside, and occasionally she got a note back; but gradually these became rarer and rarer. Soon there was little contact beyond the obligatory card at Christmas.

Almost thirteen years had passed. Uncle Joe had suffered another heart attack and died. As they had no children, Aunt Barbara now lived alone in the little house by the roadside. She was, if reports were to be believed, very frail, and never went out much; her walking days were over. In all probability, she was very lonely.

Things had changed for Sinéad too. No longer was she the wide-eyed twelve-year-old who had stood at her bedroom window looking towards the distant woodlands; at twenty-six, going on twenty-seven, she was a worldly-wise and weary woman. She had left Dublin and had gone to university in England to study history and literature, but it hadn't really worked out. After her second year, she had dropped out to marry an Englishman much older than herself, against her parents' wishes. They had stopped speaking to her, and her father had disowned her. The marriage hadn't worked out, either: after two years she and Ben had divorced and gone their separate ways.

There was no way she could go home. She had drifted for a year, taking menial jobs – clerking, waitressing, even cleaning

– first in London, then in the north of England. At last she had
summoned up the courage to return to Ireland, although not
to Dublin. She couldn't face her parents just yet. That would
take time. Her father wasn't well, and Sinéad told herself that
the inevitable confrontation would only do him harm – even
though she knew that this was only an excuse. No, after all
this time, the person she would go to – the person who still
sent her a Christmas card – was Aunt Barbara. And so she had
made her way back to County Longford. And to the wood.

Even after all this time, it seemed just as menacing, if a
little smaller than she remembered it. The dark trees still
huddled together conspiratorially along the far end of the field,
and the distant foliage was a dark, almost poisonous green.
Viewed from afar, it still gave off a distinctly unhealthy air.

But there had been changes here, too. For a start, there
had been a number of new houses built along the roadside,
near Aunt Barbara's – but, Sinéad noticed, well away from the
wood. Although the huge field had been partly turned into a
patchwork of domestic gardens, even the longest of them kept
clear of the tree-line. But the houses were grand and modern-
looking; in fact, Aunt Barbara's house was the oldest in the
area, and it looked positively shabby beside some of the flashy
bungalows that had been erected.

Aunt Barbara was just as Sinéad remembered her, however
– slightly greyer and a lot more careworn, but essentially the
same. She still wore that same old print dress – she had a
heavier, woollen version for the colder winter months – and
the same brown, sensible shoes that she had worn when Uncle
Joe was alive. And her eyes were still those of a young girl,
sparkling with mischief and anticipation. It had been her eyes
that Uncle Joe had loved most about her, he'd once told Sinéad
confidentially.

Aunt Barbara had greeted Sinéad warmly enough at the
front door of the little house, although Sinéad felt a certain
reserve and formality that she didn't remember from her

childhood. She didn't doubt that her request to come and stay with her aunt had been well discussed with her parents back in Dublin; Aunt Barbara was her mother's sister, after all. Nevertheless, behind the hesitancy, the old lady seemed genuinely delighted to see her niece once again. Sinéad had always been a bit of a favourite with her Aunt Barbara and Uncle Joe.

'Come on in.' She put her arms hesitantly round Sinéad's shoulders to give her a hint of a hug. 'You must be fairly worn out with all that travelling. Give me a moment and I'll bring your cases in. We can't have last week's washing sitting on the doorstep.' That was so like Aunt Barbara, always fussing over some little detail. But the mischievous twinkle was back in her eyes.

'No, Aunty' – Sinéad hadn't used that name in a long time – 'I'll bring them in myself. You're looking well. How're you feeling?'

The twinkle vanished momentarily, and Sinéad suspected that her aunt's health hadn't been good.

'Oh, not too bad. I was saying to your mother....' As if she realised that she'd strayed into forbidden territory, Aunt Barbara – perhaps deliberately – let the sentence hang awkwardly. 'But never mind. I've the kettle on. A cup of tea is always a great soother. Have you heard from Dermot recently at all?'

Sinéad hadn't heard from her brother in years – not since there'd been the family division over Ben – and she guessed that her aunt already half-knew the situation. But the old lady was trying to get a feel for the way the land was lying. And who was she to complain? Hadn't Aunt Barbara agreed to take her in for a while when nobody else would?

'I haven't heard from him for a wee while. I think he's still in Cork.'

Her aunt nodded. 'Just so,' she answered, as if she'd known all along.

They had reached the kitchen, and a kettle was singing

merrily on the dark range. The kitchen was more or less as Sinéad remembered it. There were a few changes – a new coat of paint, a television in the corner, some new furniture here and there – but the layout was exactly the same; the same ancient framed print of a tower window set amongst flowing greenery, with a lady looking down as if at some unseen admirer on the ground below, hung on the wall; there was the same black tea-caddy, the little clock and the two china cats on the shelf above the range, that she remembered so well.

'Children, families – they're all the same,' Aunt Barbara was saying. 'One minute they're behind you, and the next minute they're away somewhere else, with never a backward glance. Well, I suppose that's the way of the world nowadays. Now you'll take a wee sup before we go up to your old room, Sinéad.'

It was like a homecoming; although her aunt was still a little awkward and aloof, Sinéad felt as though she was where she belonged. The years and misery seemed to roll away like a blanket, and a gradual warmth crept into the kitchen, not only from the open door of the black range.

The talk was very general; Aunt Barbara skilfully avoided any probing and hurtful questions, though Sinéad imagined that these would come later. Much of the talk was about changes in the house, in the countryside, amongst former friends whom Sinéad had known when she had stayed with her aunt and uncle.

'Ah, poor Joe's death was very unexpected.... I got the television for myself soon after – he'd never have had it in the house.... The radio was always great company.... That Ryan boy that used to have a bit of an eye at you –' ('He did not,' countered Sinéad, blushing hotly.) '– well, he's married now anyhow and has seven of a family.... And the old Daly brothers that lived across the fields, both of them are long dead, God rest them....'

'I see there's been a great bit of building round here,' Sinéad said. 'New bungalows everywhere. If you don't watch out, they'll soon be uprooting the old wood to build more. That's what they're doing in England.'

Although Aunt Barbara's eyes were still kindly, her smile suddenly held all the frostiness of winter. 'Oh, I don't think they'll do that. It can never be sold. It's part of an old estate-ground.'

Sinéad gave a snort. 'That'll not stop them! You want to see what the developers are up to over in England. Destroy first and ask for planning permission later – that's what'll happen here before long.'

'They'll never touch that wood,' replied Aunt Barbara, with a curious finality in her tone. 'I did hear that Dermot was thinking of getting engaged. Have you met the girl – Anne, I think her name was? He was here, you know, last year – called in on his way up north – and he told me....'

The subject was changed, and the rest of the time was spent in gossip that circled family matters. It was a subtle choreography, darting in and out of issues, and Sinéad had the feeling that her aunt was testing the water to see how far she could go. Doubtless, Sinéad would get some sort of lecture about the importance of the family before too long – but that was in the future. In the meantime, she was home – or as near home as was possible, given the circumstances.

A warm, nostalgic glow still lingered as she returned to the room that she'd occupied as a child. As in the rest of the house, very little of significance seemed to have changed. There was still the same old dresser; the wardrobe was different, as were the curtains, but the bed was the same.

And the view from the window was the same – the distant, sinister line of trees on the other side of the field, beyond the new buildings.

Sinéad unpacked her clothes and went to the old dresser to put them, still folded, into drawers. For a second, she paused and let her gaze stray towards the window. She could just about make out the wood, and she found herself wondering momentarily about her aunt's reaction to her comment about houses being built there. As for herself, she had always detested the place. Shrugging, she pulled open a dresser drawer.

Aunt Barbara had lined the drawers with old newspapers – mostly, it seemed, local papers. As Sinéad placed the clothes in the drawer, she glimpsed part of a report on a local market, something about a sporting event, a faded colour photograph of the winner at a horse show. As she moved the paper, advertisements flitted back and forth – big savings at a nearby store; have a night out at a pub-restaurant. She smiled and arranged the clothes in the drawer. Lifting a couple of sweaters from her case, she opened the second drawer. It was also lined with newspapers – more adverts ... but there was something else. Inexplicably, Sinéad froze.

It was an article that looked as if it might be part of a regular local-history feature – 'People and Places', by somebody called Ronan Casey. But it was a grainy black-and-white photograph, set on the fold of the paper, that had caught her eye. It showed an elderly man smiling nervously into the camera; and in the background was the wood across the field.

Curious, Sinéad slid the folded paper out of the drawer and spread it on top of the dresser. The feature, obviously written by a reporter, covered some of the more famous and colourful local characters of the district. The caption under the old man's photo identified him as Michael Corrigan, who had written a book on the Hudson Estate; the picture had been taken in front of Dungort Wood. It was strange, Sinéad thought – that was the first time she'd ever heard the actual name of the wood, or of the estate on which it stood. And the more she thought about it, the more she realised how seldom people had ever talked about the place. And yet, everybody in the countryside must have known its name and at least some of its history.

She read further. Most of the article was about Michael

Corrigan himself – how he had lived in the area all his life, how this small book was his first venture into publishing, how he had always taken an interest in the old estate. But then her eye fell on a chilling passage:

> *Michael's extensive knowledge of Dungort was*
> *called upon when Gardaí searched the area in the*
> *early 1950s, following the disappearance of three*
> *young girls in the vicinity of the woodlands.*

That was all; but it was enough to send a brief chill down Sinéad's spine. She opened the paper further and checked the date – it was a year old. Crossing to the window, she looked out to see the tree-line waving in the distance – it looked even more sinister now – and some cattle huddled near the houses, well away from the wood. The feature in the newspaper only served to confirm her childhood fears about the place – that it was somehow evil and terrifying, that both humans and animals stayed well clear of it.

She refolded the newspaper and placed it back in the drawer. In a moment the photo was covered by her jumpers and a skirt, and she couldn't see it any more. For some reason, the memory of it didn't go away.

◈

Aunt Barbara half-dozed in front of the open range, trying to stay in touch with the conversation. It was clear to Sinéad that her aunt had little interest in the goings-on in London, or any of the English towns, and that her world practically stopped at the crossroads five or six miles away. Sinéad asked questions about people whom she only half-remembered from her childhood, and her aunt only partially answered: they were dead, they'd gone away, they'd had children, they still lived close by. The drowsy interchange gave them both a sense of comfort and belonging, like looking at old family photographs before going to bed.

'What was the name of that boy that used to come round here – Sean Hayles, was it?' Sinéad pulled a memory from somewhere in the past.

Aunt Barbara nodded. 'The wee boy that used to pull your hair and rub dirt on your dress?' Sinéad felt herself blushing again. 'Ah, he's a parish priest in Tralee now.'

'Go on!' answered Sinéad in surprise. 'He never is.'

Aunt Barbara nodded, half-smiling. 'And a great priest he is, too. I was talking to one of his uncles a few days ago – Malachy that lives over by the cross – and they're saying great things about him. They say he might even be a bishop....' And she sank once more into a cosy reverie.

'And there was an old man....' Seeing her aunt's guard was down, Sinéad slipped in the reference. 'I seem to remember – was it Michael Corrigan, or O'Corrigan....'

Caught momentarily, her aunt smiled to herself. 'Oh yes, old Michael. He's still living, but he's not so well. His mind wanders a bit sometimes, and he takes turns. They say that he got a fright about a year ago, and that he hasn't been the same since; but he's very old. He imagines things nowadays.'

'He wrote a book, didn't he?' Sinéad followed her first question cleverly. 'Something on the history of the district.'

Aunt Barbara jerked out of her reverie, as if she'd suddenly realised that Sinéad was angling for information.

'So he did,' she said sharply. 'And there's some round here think that he should never have done it. There's things that are best left alone – old things, best-forgotten things. It was meddling in these that gave him the fright, they say....'

She yawned loudly, her usual manner returning. 'And now I think it's time I was in bed. I get tired very easily since Joe died.'

✢

The dream was one of those that are vivid at the time but can't really be remembered once the sleeper has woken. Sinéad was walking through the wood, following a narrow path that twisted in and out of the trees. She was walking quite quickly, as though she knew her route, even though she'd never been closer to the wood than the field behind her aunt's house.

All the same, she had the sensation that someone – or something – kept pace with her, just out of her sight. Here and there, little tracks led off deeper into the woodlands, between bushes or great clumps of rhododendrons; and, as she passed the mouth of each one, a sudden movement would catch her eye, as though somebody had hurried across the intervening space and become lost in the forest once more. She could never see who or what it was. Over some of the tracks, the neighbouring tree-branches hung very low, creating patches of shadow and half-light that made it even more difficult to see if it was a person or an animal.

'Hello?' she called. 'Is there anybody there? Show yourself. Don't be afraid!' She stopped at one of the openings and peered into the gloom. There were only flitting shadows and trampled tree-mulch to see along the trail; it seemed to stretch away into darkness.

Someone touched her from behind, making her whirl round in alarm. Aunt Barbara stood there, somehow old and wasted and deathly pale, with great pools of blackness where her eyes should have been. The old woman stretched out her thin hand to grip her niece's arm.

'Three girls have gone missing in this wood,' she said in a sad, faraway voice. 'Michael Corrigan and the Gardaí are looking for them. This used to be part of the Hudson Estate, you know. Sometimes you can hear singing in the wood, very lovely singing.' She paused, as though remembering something, and the surrounding trees bowed down to hear what she had to say. 'Sean Hayles came to see me yesterday – you remember, Sinéad, the wee boy that used to pull your hair. He's a priest in Tralee now, you know. The Gardaí are still looking for them because Michael Corrigan got a fright, deep in the wood. He should have left the old Hudsons alone, never wrote about them at all. That's what everybody says.'

There was a rustling nearby; Sinéad turned, but saw nothing. When she turned back, her aunt had gone and she was alone on the forest path.

'Aunt Barbara?' she called. 'Aunt Barbara!'

There were whispers and mutterings from the forest all around her, as though an unseen host of people went back and forth on the other side of the trees. She thought she heard a little girl crying, somewhere close at hand.

'Aunt Barbara? Where are you?'

She woke with daylight creeping around the edges of the curtains in her room, and the dream faded and was gone completely. But she remembered that she'd dreamt, and that it had had something to do with the wood.

The sound of a radio filled the kitchen as she came downstairs. Aunt Barbara was bustling by the range, making a fried breakfast – something Sinéad hadn't eaten in years and had no real desire to eat now. But, to please her aunt, she would try; the old lady meant well.

'Best meal o' the day,' said Aunt Barbara, scraping fried egg from the bottom of a black pan – Sinéad's stomach lurched a bit. 'A good breakfast will have you ready for whatever the world wants to throw at you.'

Sinéad ate slowly and without much relish, washing every mouthful down with hot tea. On the other side of the table, her aunt pecked, hen-like, at some lightly buttered toast. 'I'm not one to eat much in the mornings since Joe died. But he liked a hearty breakfast, all right.' Sinéad could have pointed out that it might have been too many 'hearty breakfasts' that had finally killed him, but she didn't.

The talk took up where it had left off the night before – local characters, changed places – punctuated by periods of silence when the radio took over. As the news came on, Aunt Barbara signalled that she wanted to listen to it; like many old ladies, she seemed very set in her ways. Sinéad pushed bacon and remnants of egg to the side of her plate.

'Gardaí are still searching for an eight-year-old girl who disappeared on Tuesday near her Tallaght home in Dublin,' said the newscaster. 'No trace of the girl, who has been named as Mary O'Connor, has been found, despite extensive enquiries in the area where she was last seen playing with some friends. Inspector Sean Crossley, leading the enquiry, said last night....'

'Didn't some girls disappear round here at one stage?' said Sinéad suddenly. Her aunt turned, as if waking from a dream, and there was a hint of fear in her eyes. 'I remember reading about it. In the 1950s, wasn't it? And weren't the Gardaí brought in here too? You and Uncle Joe must have been living here around then.'

Aunt Barbara seemed to be thinking quickly. 'I remember something of the kind,' she said at last. 'But not very much. Your uncle would have been able to tell you more about it. He was in the search party that went into the wood to look for Kitty Ryan when she ... went away.' She seemed uncomfortable with the memory.

'And Kitty Ryan was ...?' Sinéad persisted.

'One of the wee girls who's supposed to have gone into the wood,' her aunt said swiftly and a trifle sharply, Sinéad thought. 'Nobody ever found her. The Guards said she was dead, but nobody knew for sure. She was a stupid, giddy girl – I called her a wee girl, but she must have been in her teens. Some people said she'd been taken by the fairies – but that was just an oul' superstition. A couple of other girls vanished, too, but I can't remember their names now – if Joe had been here, he could have told you. One of them was a niece of Michael Corrigan's. That's why the Guards brought him in.'

'And they went into the wood as well?' asked Sinéad, intrigued.

Aunt Barbara seemed genuinely thrown by the question. 'So they said. Of course, no one ever really knew for certain, but it was thought that they had. The wood had a fearsome reputation in those days – it was no more than a lot of oul' superstition, but people believed it.'

'And what was the story?' Sinéad persisted; but her aunt waved her away.

'Oh, I can't remember it all now – something about ghosts, something connected to the oul' Hudsons that used to own the estate. That was their wood at a time. And they were a bad lot – had no regard for the people round about. But I can't rightly mind. Your Uncle Joe could've told you; he was always into oul' stories and nonsense like that.' She clearly had no wish to discuss the subject any further. 'Now, Sinéad, I've been meaning to ask you – has your mother been in contact since…. It's only that she said to me that she might, now you're back. I think she'd like to talk to you, anyway….'

It was a clever ploy – if it was a ploy – to divert the talk away from the wood, and it worked: Sinéad momentarily found herself at a loss for words. Then, suddenly, the dam broke, as it had been waiting to do, and slowly it all came out – the break-up of her marriage, the difficulty of a young woman living with an older man, his business commitments ensuring that he was never home, how she had been stuck in a town where she knew nobody, her desire to return to Ireland, her father's hot words when he had disowned her…. She talked for the best part of an hour, while her aunt nodded sympathetically. For the moment, all thoughts of the wood were gone.

Sinéad cried for a while, and then went for a walk. She knew that her eyes were puffed up and red, but she needed to get out and let a good, brisk stroll – just a walk along the road, going nowhere special – take away all the hurt and anxiety she felt.

It was good to revisit the places she'd known as a child,

even if many of them had changed. The narrow, slate-roofed cottage where a little woman named Mary Rogan had lived was gone, and there was a large modern bungalow in the field behind where it had stood. Sinéad seemed to remember Aunt Barbara telling her that Mary Rogan had died years ago and her land had been sold. An old two-storey house, once owned by a family called Kelly, now stood half-ruined and open to the world, the glass gone from its windows and the peeling front door hanging on its hinges. Sinéad stopped thoughtfully, remembering what it had been like when it was full of the noise of all the Kelly children. Frankie Kelly had never worked a day in his life, but he had always seemed to have money, and he had had more children than she could count – all, apparently, gone now.

As she turned away, she looked across the fields on the other side of the road. The distant tree-line waved back at her, and she suddenly realised something she'd never recognised all those years ago: the whole road was dominated by Dungort Wood, just across the fields. There was no getting away from it. She noticed one other thing, too. Normally, in woodlands, riots of birds would occasionally rise squalling into the air; but not at Dungort. True, there were a few crows in the sky above the trees, but they seemed to wheel and veer as if turning away from something, and they never seemed to settle amongst the trees. It was odd, Sinéad thought, but probably not inexplicable. Dungort – even the name sounded a wee bit sinister....

Rounding a bend, she came on somebody standing by a roadside gate, looking out across the fields to the woodland. He leaned heavily on the iron top bar, and she saw a stick propped against the bars beside him. Somehow he seemed familiar.

Then she realised. The photo had been grainy and ill-defined, but she still recognised Michael Corrigan from the newspaper in the drawer. He looked older and much frailer;

but then, she supposed, the photo had been taken over a year ago. Should she speak to him? Maybe not. Best to go on.

However, as she drew level with him, the old man half-turned, showing her a thin, grey face that almost matched the colour of his fading hair.

'Hello,' Sinéad said, and made to walk on. There was something about his eyes, which dominated his face, that she didn't like. They were wild and frightened, like those of a man who had seen something terrible.

'He got a bit of a fright....' Aunt Barbara's words echoed somewhere in the back of her mind. *'It was his own fault. Should have left things alone.'*

'There used to be an old mill a little ways on along this road, down by the Glarry Burn,' Michael Corrigan said suddenly, without preamble. 'Run by a man called Colm Sweeny. Sweeny's Mill, they called it hereabouts, but it was pulled down just after the First World War. The British thought the Republicans were using it for storing weapons after the 1916 Rising.' And he turned back to look at the far-off wood again. 'You used to be able to see some of the old walls of it.'

Sinéad remembered that. As a child, she had played among the stumps of old walls peeping up through the roadside briars and tangled grasses. She had never known that they'd once belonged to a mill.

'Wasn't there a bridge across the stream beside it?' she asked.

He didn't turn; he kept looking steadily towards Dungort. 'There was,' he answered. 'And there used to be an old standing stone up in the fields behind it. The local people were terrified of it. They said the Devil came there on Hallowe'en night.' Slowly he turned to look at her. 'You're Margaret Rogan, aren't you – Mary Rogan's girl? I worked with your Uncle John years ago. How is your mother?'

'No, I'm not Margaret Rogan,' Sinéad answered, and started to walk on. Although his intense stare seemed intelligent enough, he was clearly confused. 'You've made a mistake, I'm afraid.'

Michael Corrigan gave a high, unpleasant laugh, turning squarely to face her. 'Of course you're not! You're Bridget Burke. You know, people thought you were lost in the wood and you'd never be seen again. But I knew different – I knew you'd come back. That was the way of it for them that were taken by Himself. That's what I told the Gardaí, but they wouldn't pay any heed to me.'

He moved towards Sinéad, with some difficulty, and tried to grab her arm with his skinny hand. Frightened, she took a couple of steps back. 'I seen Himself there, about a year ago – the old Hudson. Over at the edge of the wood. He comes there sometimes, right to the edge of the trees, and looks out over the countryside. That's how he took those girls away with him. Like an old man, he was. It gave me a turn to see him so close.'

His attitude changed, becoming tense – almost threatening – and his voice had fallen to a whisper, as if he was afraid to say the words. Sinéad backed slightly further away, unsure of what to expect. 'Don't go into the wood, Bridget – there's no safe path through it. And Himself is always about, waiting for girls like yourself. He waits for the hurt, the fearful, the lonely – that's what I've always heard. He's waitin' for the likes of you, Bridie. That's the truth of it. Anybody round here will tell you that!' And, clearly exhausted by his efforts, he turned away and went to lean on the gate again.

Sinéad turned on her heel and hurried back the way she'd come, upset by the queer old man and his strange warning.

☦

The shock of the encounter still hadn't left her several hours later, as her aunt made her something to eat. That was all Aunt Barbara seemed to do – maybe it was all she had ever done: cook, polish and clean, sew, make beds, arrange furniture. It seemed a lonely, sterile life, without much purpose, change or challenge. It was a life that Sinéad had thought to escape by going to university; and yet, she thought, here she was, back in her aunt's kitchen, as if she'd never been away, knowing that she hadn't really escaped at all.

'Did you meet anybody interesting out on your walk?' Aunt Barbara asked, as she cooked potatoes in a small black pot on the edge of the stove.

Sinéad nodded. 'I met that old man you were talking about – Michael Corrigan – and he mistook me for somebody else. I don't think he's all there.'

Aunt Barbara nodded sadly. 'Poor Michael. His mind's usually away with it. I don't know how his daughter puts up with him, now that her husband's dead – he lives with her, in that big farmhouse just beyond Tully Cross. It's his grand age – he's over ninety, you know – and the fright he got about a year ago. He hasn't been the same since.'

Sinéad nodded, suddenly sensing something in her aunt's tone. 'He said something about it – about somebody coming to the edge of the wood and looking out through the trees. Somebody he called "Himself", or one of the old Hudsons. I think that's what frightened him. Do you know anything about it?'

Aunt Barbara sniffed loudly. 'Old nonsense. Some of the stuff he put in that silly book that he wrote. Your Uncle Joe read it out to me one time, but I can't rightly remember what it was all about.'

Sinéad looked at her enquiringly, and the old woman hesitated. 'It … it might have been about one of the Hudson landowners. They were a bad lot – they'd held these lands since the days of Cromwell, and they were greatly hated – but there was one of them, I can't rightly remember his name, who was worse than all the others. They said he sold his soul to the Devil in a sort of shooting lodge or something in Dungort

Wood.' It was the first time Sinéad had heard her aunt mention the wood by name. 'He's supposed to be buried up there. But the likes of Michael Corrigan would tell you that he's not really dead, that he's over there among the trees, like some sort of ghost. When those silly girls went away, in the 50s, there was a lot of oul' superstitious talk that they'd been carried away into the wood. There was even some talk about blood-drinking and all that nonsense. I think they ran off somewhere and were never got.' There was a finality in the last few words that told Sinéad that Aunt Barbara didn't want to talk about the subject any more.

Her tone lightened. 'I've asked Father McCarthy to call round and meet you. He said he'd maybe come round either today or tomorrow – he's a very busy man. Maybe you could talk to him about....' She let the sentence trail off awkwardly.

Sinéad hadn't seen a priest in years (Ben had been a lapsed Anglican, as he'd been fond of telling everyone), let alone an Irish country priest. She'd been told that such men wielded great power in the country parishes, that their word was law. Doubtless Aunt Barbara thought that a word from the priest would force Sinéad into some sort of reconciliation with her parents. The old woman meant well, but she had another thing coming. Sinéad decided that she would contrive to be out when Father Whatever-his-name-was arrived, even if it meant staying out for most of the day. However, she smiled graciously at her aunt as she served up the potatoes.

The afternoon was truly glorious – one of those that invite a walk. Sinéad had to get out of the house, in case the priest should arrive, so she told her aunt that she would take a short after-dinner stroll and be back shortly.

She walked for longer than she could have imagined – well beyond the crossroads that she knew as Tully Cross – and found herself on a steep incline, heading towards the crest of a low hill. The roads were long and empty, with only scattered houses here and there – some obviously uninhabited or in ruins – separated by sour, desolate fields or copses of dark trees. And no matter where she went, she could still see Dungort.

No car had passed her on the lonely road, nor had she met another person. However, as she began to climb the hill, a priest came hurtling down the road on a bicycle, his coat flapping behind him like great black wings. He smiled as he passed Sinéad, and she smiled back, wondering if he was on his way to Aunt Barbara's.

She climbed onward. Below her the land began to spread out, and she could see the poverty of the place – sad, narrow fields; roads that seemed to lead nowhere; clumps of trees and lone standing stones; squat stone dwellings dotted away amongst the hollows in the land. And there, too, was the wood, spreading like a sinister mantle of green across the edges of her vision. It reminded her for a moment of her aunt's hesitant story about the place, and of Michael Corrigan's strange warning.

'I don't know how his daughter puts up with him, now that her husband's dead,' Aunt Barbara's voice echoed somewhere in the back of her mind. *'In that big farmhouse just beyond Tully Cross....'* Looking around, Sinéad wondered if she was anywhere near the old man's house. Maybe she could call in to him, get him to explain further about the wood.

Maybe not. Maybe she was better off not knowing too much – her aunt certainly seemed to think so. But if she were to go back now, she might very well run into the priest, Father What's-his-name, and she didn't want that.

She stopped at a roadside cottage and asked the woman who answered the door if Michael Corrigan lived locally. The woman pointed to a large black-stone farmhouse on a rise just down the road, at the end of a laneway. That was Michael Corrigan's house, she said. Almost instinctively, Sinéad turned towards its gate.

The old man sat in the sun on a low chair, near a little

wooden porch at the front of the house. He appeared to be almost asleep, dozing in the late-afternoon heat. As Sinéad's shadow fell across him, he opened his large eyes and looked at her quizzically.

'I seen you before,' he said suddenly. 'You're Bridie Burke that went away years ago. They looked for you all over the countryside, and they thought you were dead or lost. But I knew different. Them that goes to live with Himself in the wood never dies. They live forever, an' I knew you'd come back, Bridie.'

'You're wrong, Mr Corrigan. I'm not Bridget Burke, I'm Sinéad Mo – Sinéad Farrell.' She almost used her married name but caught herself just in time. 'I used to spend the summers with my aunt, Barbara Horan, down on the other side of Tully Cross.'

Whether he had heard her or not, her words didn't seem to register with him. 'I warned the other one – that Kitty Ryan – after you'd gone. Don't go near Dungort Wood, I said to her. Not when Himself is about, all through the trees.'

He paused. 'You don't remember the oul' house, do you, Bridie? I barely mind it myself, and I'm a great bit older than you. But a grand place it was altogether. They pulled it down long years ago, but it was a great house in its day. I seen it myself as a child. The old Hudsons lived there and owned the lands all through Dungort. They would go hunting in the wood, Bridie, and they built a kind of shooting lodge there.' He was warming to his tale. 'And one of them more or less lived there. But a bad crowd they were – bad cess to them all, every one.'

He suddenly spat onto the ground, and Sinéad had to step backwards to avoid it. 'And that one that lived in the shooting lodge, he was the worst of them all. He became a kind o' hermit, never went near the big house, lived away in the wood. He was a strange man. It was said that he'd sold his soul to the Devil and that he did terrible things in the lodge.

'It was a tinker man that found him dead – he was an old

man by that time, an' even more strange in his ways – and they buried him without too much fuss. He was so hated by the people round about that no monument stands to him in the churchyard.' He leaned forward in his chair in an almost confidential manner. 'There's them that say he wasn't buried in the churchyard at all, because the people and the Church wouldn't have it, but that he lies out in the wood.

'Then queer stories began to grow up. It was said that oul' Hudson was often seen moving through the wood, just as he did when he was alive. Sometimes he would come as an old man, just as he had been in his last days, leaning on a stick and limping between the trees; but at other times he was a youngster, walking very quickly among the bushes. He had the glamour, d'ye see, like the fairies. They can make ye see anything they want, an' then can take on any shape or form.

'Queer things began to happen round about. Cows started fallin' in the fields and had blood drained from their necks. They never rose again. Everybody said it was the ghost o' the oul' Squire Hudson in the wood that was drinkin' it. He was doin' terrible things in death, just as he had in life. People became very afraid o' the wood, and nobody would go near it – nor even talk about it, in case Himself would hear. That's what I told Kitty Ryan, Bridie. But she never listened.'

'I'm not Bridie, Mr Corrigan,' Sinéad reminded him. 'But who was this Squire Hudson? Why did he take away the three girls?'

Michael Corrigan, however, had drifted onto some other topic in a low, meandering tone. 'Do you remember Daniel Sullivan? He was your grandfather, wasn't he, Maureen? I mind when he owned the oul' forge down at the Cross. He was a quick-tempered man, but a kindly one as well. I remember when he brought you up on his shoulder, Maureen, down at Lannigan's pub. You were only a wee thing....'

'Father!' A shrill voice cut the old man's ramblings off in mid-flow. 'What have I told you about speaking to strangers?'

A sharp-featured, plain woman was walking briskly – no, half-running – from the house in their direction. 'Can I help you?' The question was aimed at Sinéad, like a command.

The arrival of his daughter seemed to concentrate the old man's mind. 'It's Himself, Bridie – one of the *marbh bheo* – the walking, blood-drinking dead. That's what I told the Guards, but they never heeded me.'

The woman had positioned herself between her father and Sinéad, her arms folded. She was perhaps younger than she looked, but her hair was streaked with grey and her face looked washed-out and worn.

'What is it you want with my father?' she demanded. 'I won't have him bothered by anyone. He's an old man and his mind's not what it was.'

Sinéad was floored, not knowing how to respond to the woman's aggression. 'I – I didn't ...' she began. 'I didn't mean ...'

'It's Bridie Burke, Kathleen!' said Michael Corrigan cheerily. 'She went away into the wood, but she's come back. Take her in, Kathleen, and give her some tea. I'll want to hear what she's been doing in that place. I want to hear if she met Himself!'

The woman's sour expression didn't soften; in fact, it seemed to grow harder, and her fierce, protective eyes threw out a distinct challenge to Sinéad. 'That's not Bridie Burke, Da,' she retorted, without looking at the old man. 'Bridie's dead these long years. This is somebody else.' The glare grew even harder. 'He gets confused sometimes. Now what is it that you want here?'

Sinéad was still stumped by the woman's obvious hostility. 'I ... I thought that I might speak to your father,' she blurted out at last. 'About the book that he's written. About Dungort Wood.'

The woman caught her breath, but her harsh gaze never wavered. 'He knows nothing about it,' she snapped. 'An', like

I said, he gets very confused an' doesn't make much sense. Who are you, anyway? Some sort of journalist?'

'Bridie's not dead, Kathleen,' Michael Corrigan cut across her. 'Not her, nor Kitty Ryan, nor Mary Flood. They're all with Himself in the wood.'

The woman swung on him. 'Now, Da, we'll have none o' that oul' nonsense!' She turned back to Sinéad. 'All this talk o' Dungort Wood only upsets him. He got a bad scare there over a year ago, and he hasn't been well since. If you're a journalist, I'll thank you to be on your way. In fact, if you've no other business here, I'll thank you to be going anyway.' And there was an emphasis in her tone that brooked no argument.

Sinéad backed away. 'I … I'm sorry … I didn't mean to….' The words came out in a garble. The old man in the chair had fallen silent; he seemed to be concentrating on something far away over the fields. Sinéad turned and hurried back towards the laneway. Behind her she heard Michael Corrigan's voice, high and querulous, and his daughter's sullen replies.

On the way back to her aunt's, Sinéad passed by an open gate. Away across the fields, the tree-line of Dungort Wood seemed to beckon her, and she paused. Was old Michael Corrigan merely rambling, or was there something among those distant trees, something that watched her as she hurried by? She thought about her dream. In it, someone or something had been following her, running between the aisles of trees, darting across the woodland paths. Had it been simply a nightmare, or had it been something more?

Across the field, the tops of the trees still waved invitingly. Almost involuntarily, she found herself walking through the open gateway towards them.

The way across the field was uneven and filled with potholes where cattle had been standing. Nearer the tree-line, however, the ground was firmer and less pitted, as though the animals had never ventured close to the wood but had kept a healthy distance from its edge. Sinéad half-expected to see a figure – what had the old man said? 'Himself'? – standing in the queer light under the overhanging branches, but there was nothing.

But she also noticed the silence of the place. No birdsong, no subtle movements of hidden animals scurrying away as she approached; the wood remained gloomy and silent in the late-afternoon sun. Here and there a narrow, earthen, stone-studded path disappeared into the darkened depths, but there was no movement there either. She wondered whether she should walk a little way along one of the paths.

She took a step forward. The trees closed around her like a curtain, but still nothing stirred. The woodlands seemed to be dreaming in the lazy heat. Ahead, great banks of foxgloves suddenly reared up, nodding gently at Sinéad's approach.

They marked a break in the path; beyond them, it plunged deeper into the wood, winding round on itself to become lost amongst the trees. Sinéad wondered if she should follow this track and lose herself amongst the shady greenery all around her. It was a tempting thing to do – put the world of a broken marriage, hostile parents, a nosy aunt and her priest, far behind her and just spend her time deep in the woodlands. It was a kind of running away, a rejection of the world she'd known. She'd never thought like this before.

'It's beautiful at this time of the year, isn't it?' The suddenness of the voice behind her startled her, and a little scream rose unbidden in the back of her throat as she turned.

A man was emerging from amongst the foxgloves, so close that she couldn't imagine how she had missed seeing him before. He had probably come up from one of the houses down near the edge of the road. He was a youngish man, dressed in shabby, dusty, old-fashioned clothes – a dark double-breasted jacket, wide black trousers secured by a thick leather belt, and a dirty-looking off-white shirt. Sturdy shoes made almost no sound as they came across the grass.

As he drew level with Sinéad, he gave a wide smile and slowed his pace.

'It's a grand evening for a walk,' he said, in an accent that was somewhere between thick Kerry and upper-class English, almost impossible to define. 'Are you going into the wood? It's lovely at this time of the year.' And he made a peculiar motion in the air, as if inviting her to step further along the path, into its comforting darkness.

For a second Sinéad was tempted; but then, suddenly and inexplicably, an image of her Aunt Barbara sprang into her mind – Aunt Barbara pouring tea for the priest, who was steadfastly looking at the clock on the mantelpiece. In her mind, her aunt wore an embarrassed smile. *'I'm sure Sinéad won't be much longer, Father.'* She could almost hear Aunt Barbara saying the words, somewhere in the back of her mind. *'She said she'd only be out for an hour or so.'* The priest returned the smile, but in a steely fashion; he was clearly not used to being kept waiting. Whatever Sinéad thought of priests, her aunt deserved better than to be embarrassed in front of them. She should go home and face the music.

The vision was gone, and the stranger was in front of her again.

'There's a particularly nice rhododendron bush a little way along there,' he was saying. 'Really worth seeing.'

But Sinéad shook her head and turned back. 'I don't think so,' she replied. 'Not today.'

He shrugged. 'You look as if you could do with some cheering up.' He extended a hand. 'My name's Liam, by the way.'

She took the hand; it seemed warm and comforting and full of vibrant life.

'Sinéad,' she replied. 'I used to live round here.'

Liam snorted a brief laugh. 'I still do. But haven't you just come back from England or something? I think I heard you were living with …' He searched for the name.

'My aunt,' answered Sinéad, marvelling to herself that she was actually telling him. Word certainly got around in these small communities. 'Barbara Horan.' In the brassy, fading light, his face seemed younger and his smile was very fetching.

'Ah, yes,' he said. 'I should know her, but I don't think I do. Are you staying long?'

She smiled, not anxious to tell him too much. He'd probably find out from some of the locals, anyway. 'A wee while. I'm not sure yet.'

She suddenly realised that, while they'd been talking, the pair of them had been walking further into the wood. At the clump of foxgloves they'd taken the path that wound deeper into the woodlands; now they were walking into a shady part where the branches threw odd, dappled shadows everywhere. 'Look, I really have to be getting back. It was lovely to meet you, Liam. Maybe we'll run into each other again soon.'

He seemed disappointed, even a touch angry, but nonetheless he smiled. 'Sure,' he said. 'It was grand to meet you, too, Sinéad. I've no doubt that we'll meet up again before too long.'

She turned and hurried back towards the edge of the trees, noting that he made no attempt to follow her. He was just standing in the shade of a large tree, and as she stole a backward glance, she saw him turn away into the woodland gloom. Amongst the tree-shadows, he seemed a little older than she had thought. Was that a moustache across his upper lip? No, it must have been a trick of the light.

And it was best not to pay him too much attention. Leaving the wood behind her, Sinéad hurried across the open field, through the gate and onto the road once more.

✦

'There is still no trace of eight-year-old Mary O'Connor, who vanished from her Tallaght home last Tuesday,' the tones of Aunt Barbara's radio greeted Sinéad as she stole into the kitchen. *'Gardaí have switched their investigations from the area in which she was last seen playing to several nearby deserted premises, leading to speculation that she might have been abducted. In an appeal for witnesses regarding her last movements, Inspector Sean Crossley, leading the investigation, stated …'*

Aunt Barbara was alone in the kitchen, mashing potatoes for the evening meal. If the priest had been there, he was gone. Aunt Barbara looked up and shot Sinéad a dark glance as she came into the kitchen.

'Father McCarthy waited for over an hour for you,' she reported icily. 'You said you'd only be a short while. Where were you?'

Sinéad looked suitably chastened. 'I … I'm sorry. I walked further than I thought – got talking to people…. I didn't notice the time….'

'But you knew that Father McCarthy was coming!' Aunt Barbara's voice was angry now. Sinéad had been right: the priest wasn't used to being kept waiting. 'It was bad manners not to come home to meet him!' There was a hint of outrage in her aunt's tone: how dared she flout a priest in such a cavalier fashion? 'Who were you talking to, anyway, that took up so much of your time?' The question positively dripped sarcasm.

'I met Michael Corrigan,' Sinéad answered.

Her aunt snorted. 'That oul' eejit – I'm sure you got plenty of sense out of *him*! He doesn't know what day of the week it is half the time! I don't know how that daughter of his puts up with him – always wandering away and prowling round those oul' woodlands. And you wasted your time talking to him! Is *that* who you were with when Father McCarthy was waiting for you?'

'No. I met somebody called Liam….' Sinéad didn't want to

admit that she'd been anywhere near Dungort Wood. 'I think
he was from one of the new bungalows down along the roadside. A youngish man, shabbily dressed, but very pleasant.'

Her aunt tutted disapprovingly. 'That'll be Liam Rogan,
old Mary Rogan's youngest boy. He's sometimes as addled as
oul' Michael Corrigan. Although he has a fair penny behind
him, I'm told. Oul' Mary was careful with the money, and
there's only himself and another sister – the eldest brother
died before the mother did. That's how he can afford to live in
those new bungalows. He's pleasant enough, I suppose, but
he's a strange character, always hanging about the roads. You
never know what he's up to, I say. And to think that you passed
up a meeting with Father McCarthy for those two!' She was
clearly very displeased. 'Still, not to worry – I've asked him to
call round tomorrow evening, when you're in. Talking to him
will suit you better than hearing nonsense from the likes of
Liam Rogan or Michael Corrigan.' And there was such finality
in her tone that Sinéad didn't dare argue with her.

⊕

The dream was back that night. This time she was running
through the wood, while someone kept pace with her behind
a bank of trees and foxgloves. She tried to see who it was, but
the foliage kept getting in the way; she could only make out
an indistinct shape, running parallel to her.

'Hello?' she called, hearing her own voice echoing back
from the trees around her. 'Is there anybody there?' It was a
silly question, for she could see the darting shape through the
foliage; but this was a dream – wasn't it? – and you were
allowed to do and say silly things in dreams.

There was, of course, no answer. The thing, whatever it
was, seemed to disappear deeper into the woodlands.

Sinéad rounded a bend in the trail, and a massive bank of
foxgloves reared in front of her. There was something off to

her left – a clearing, with what looked like a large stone in the centre. Even as she turned to look at it, she was aware of a movement among the foxgloves. A dark shadow sprang at her.

With a scream, she stumbled back. Someone caught her from behind. Half-turning, she saw that it was Liam, and that the dark thing that had jumped at her had disappeared.

Liam smiled reassuringly. 'There's nothing to be afraid of now,' he whispered softly.

There was another movement in the middle of the fox-gloves, as if something was readying itself to spring again. Sinéad turned to see who or what it was ... and woke up.

Early-morning sunlight streamed into the room. She rose, half-stupidly, the last vestiges of the dream clearing from her mind, and went to the window. Throwing back the curtains, she admitted the sun fully to her room.

A hare was gambolling across the field outside her window, darting in the direction of the bungalows. Away in the distance, Dungort Wood waved good morning to her. A couple of birds wheeled above it, but none of them alighted. From somewhere downstairs, she could hear the faint sound of her aunt's radio; it sounded like the news. The dream faded and broke into fragments, only shards of which Sinéad could remember: the endless running along a stony path ... someone keeping pace with her.... Pulling on her clothes, she went downstairs.

'They've found that wee girl, the one in Tallaght,' Aunt Barbara greeted her as she came into the kitchen. 'She's dead. They think she was killed by somebody that knew her.'

Sinéad listened, but the newscaster had moved on to something about the Irish economy. 'An awful thing!' Aunt Barbara was saying. 'She was no more than about eight or nine, just like wee Maeve Foley that lives down below Joyce's. I kept imagining it was Maeve, and that they'd have to bring out the searchers, like they did before when your Uncle Joe went with them. It must be terrible for her parents – that's what I was saying to Father McCarthy only yesterday.' She clattered about the kitchen, shaking her head, while Sinéad laid the table for breakfast.

'By the way, the Father's coming round this evening, so don't be wandering off like you did yesterday.' There was both warning and reproach in the tone, and Sinéad knew no further excuses would be tolerated.

They spent breakfast in general chatter, with Aunt Barbara reading from the local paper and explaining about people that she used to know. She said that she had to visit a neighbour woman down the road, and invited Sinéad to come. Sinéad declined; she wanted to visit some of her old haunts. Aunt Barbara agreed, with repeated warnings about not being late for Father McCarthy. The priest, Sinéad guessed, would not be kept waiting a second time.

Nevertheless, for some strange reason, by afternoon Sinéad found herself walking across the fields. In a fit of self-indulgent nosiness, she found herself inspecting the backs and the little gardens of the bungalows that had been built along the side of the road, wondering who lived in them. In one or two gardens, washing flapped on the line, although the day threatened rain. A dog stood at the back door of one house, barking loudly, as she passed by. But there was no sign of human life anywhere. Which of these houses did the mysterious Liam live in? she wondered.

To avoid a flock of sheep – which still scared her a little – she walked halfway across a field, closer to the wood. Was it her imagination, or was there someone standing amongst the trees, watching her? Yes, there was, she was sure of it; and from a distance it looked like old Michael Corrigan. She should go and apologise to the old man for upsetting him and his daughter the previous day, she thought; she turned her footsteps towards the edge of the trees.

The figure seemed to move a little way back into the woodland, but Sinéad could still see him. A curious sheep ran out to her left, and instinctively she turned to look at it; when she looked back, the figure amongst the trees was gone. However, she could still feel that someone was watching her, keeping pace with her progress across the field. It had to be Michael Corrigan; she had seen him, surely, among the trees. She approached the edge of the woodland warily.

'Mr Corrigan?' she called. Somewhere overhead, a wheeling bird answered her call, but the wood itself remained silent.

Sinéad came to the very edge of the trees. The inner gloom looked inviting, but she could see nobody. Something or someone rustled in the undergrowth – was that a movement, or simply a twig falling somewhere ahead of her? Then the wood was silent once more.

'Hello? Mr Corrigan?' She took a few tentative steps between the trees. Gloom wrapped itself about her like a comforting cloak.

The sound came again, this time from somewhere close at hand, and she thought she saw a movement out of the corner of her eye. Someone was moving through the undergrowth to her left. She had a quick glimpse of a bowed form – an old man, badly stooped, with greying hair. It had to be Michael Corrigan. But he was suddenly gone, under an overhanging branch and out of her sight.

Perhaps he was confused, Sinéad told herself. He had mistaken her for somebody else and maybe he was frightened. She should get him back and set him on the road home.

'Mr Corrigan!' She darted after him, unmindful that she was walking further into the woodland. 'It's me. You met me yesterday....'

She found herself hurrying along an earthen path. Overhead, the day seemed to darken slightly, although that might simply have been due to the branches above her; a breeze, slight but cold, seemed to spring up from the very heart of the wood. At a large clump of foxgloves that waved purple heads at her approach, she paused, unsure what way to go.

A sound to her left, on the path that led further into the gloom, made her turn and hurry in its direction; she thought she saw part of a stooped back disappearing amongst the foliage ahead, but she couldn't be sure. Trees clustered thickly everywhere, towering above her menacingly, like ragged sentinels protecting some awful secret. Quickening her pace, she brushed aside low branches and tall, stinging nettles.

The trail suddenly emerged into a wider pathway, which seemed to plunge directly towards the very heart of the wood. Grass grew along its middle and tall weeds flanked its sides, their white heads nodding slightly, like those of old men, in the breeze that seemed to travel along its length. It was badly overgrown but still passable. It was also completely deserted; if Sinéad had expected to see Michael Corrigan, she was disappointed. Where could the old man have gone?

Without really thinking about it, she turned her steps towards the woodland's heart, looking around for him. There was no sign. Trees rose imperiously on either side; small avenues of near-dark, where the light struggled to penetrate their branches, disappeared into the depths. Here and there, she could see glimmers of brilliance where they emerged into the sunlight again. Pale fronds waved at her; great bunches of nettles nodded warningly.

She walked on a little further, but she met no one. Even the birdsong of the morning had stopped. The wind was freshening, so much that it threatened to become a minor gale. Shadows lengthened and, although it was still far from evening, a gradual darkness seemed to be stealing across Dungort Wood. Why she didn't turn and walk back to the wood's edge, Sinéad didn't know; it was almost as if something compelled her to explore further and deeper among the trees. Ducking between trailing briars, low branches, and clusters of nettles, she walked on. From somewhere amid the dense growth around her, she heard faint sounds, maybe a branch falling – or might it be something moving through the undergrowth, stealthily keeping pace with her?

'Hello?' she shouted again. The only answer was the echo of her own call from the wall of trees on either side. 'Is there anybody there?' Not even a bird answered her cry. She felt suddenly afraid, and chided herself for coming into the woodland at all.

In front, the path rounded a bend over some low branches and vanished into almost-total darkness. A breeze caught the edges of Sinéad's hair and ruffled it. She wondered if it would be wise to go any further. Turning, she looked back the way she'd come. Darkness was crawling towards her down the path behind, and she wondered what was more frightening – the advancing gloom or the dark in front. This must be how those three girls felt when they came into Dungort, she told herself.

She decided to go on a little further. If the old man was there, they could leave together. Warily she advanced, past the large upturned root of a tree, seeing the bend of the path open up before her to reveal more trees huddled along its edges. On the other side of the bend it twisted again, up a slight incline and out into the sunlight once more. Sinéad hurried through the darkness of interlocking branches and out into the open, finding herself in a clearing near the very centre of the wood.

Although the area, free of encroaching trees as it was, should have been bright and sunny, a kind of ominous gloom hung over it like a shadow. Sinéad noticed that it was very cold – colder, she thought, than anywhere else in the woodland. The clearing was just a wide, open, overgrown space, flanked on all sides by trees and filled with tufts of nettles and brambles and the inevitable clusters of foxgloves and rhododendrons. Here the path came to an abrupt end, lost in the tall grasses and undergrowth of the clearing.

Everything was very still as Sinéad took a few steps forward, her way obstructed by the weeds. Apart from herself, the clearing was empty. If Michael Corrigan was in this wood, he wasn't here.

She was turning back towards the path when something,

half-hidden by grass and foxgloves, caught her eye. It looked very much like a small standing stone, but it was so obscured by foliage that she might well have missed it. Something impelled her to walk towards it, ignoring the thorns that tried to catch her legs and the nettles that seemed to bend down to sting her.

It was no more than a large stone – maybe a rock or boulder that had been dumped there in some former time – but, as she looked at it, Sinéad thought that there was writing across the broad flatness of its top. No, it was probably no more than a series of cracks in the stone itself – and yet they looked like letters. What did they spell? *H-U-D*.... No, they weren't letters at all....

'Hello.' A voice behind her made her turn, expecting to see Michael Corrigan emerging from amongst the trees. But it was not an old man's voice.

He was standing behind her, as though he'd been watching her for a long time. Liam, dressed as he had been before – the same shabby clothes, the same workman's boots. 'I see you've found my secret place, then.' He began to cross the clearing towards her, taking giant, awkward steps to avoid the clumps of grass. 'I sometimes come here to get away from things. Maybe you're doing the same. But you're very welcome, anyway.'

And he was beside her. Sinéad thought for a second that she smelt something vaguely unpleasant, like a passing foul breath full on her face, but then it was gone again.

'I got a bit lost,' she blurted out. 'I thought I saw somebody that I sort of half-knew – an old man I was talking to yesterday – but maybe I was mistaken.'

Liam's smile was disarming. 'Easy enough done – getting lost, I mean. There's all sorts of paths through this wood. Most of 'em lead here; I think there used to be an old building here, but there's no trace of it now. It's a very peaceful spot here, anyway.'

It was certainly quiet, but Sinéad didn't like the way the

shadows moved and wove across the open ground, creating their own particular darkness.

'It was a man called Michael Corrigan that I was looking for,' she told Liam. 'Do you know him? He's an old man who used to write about this wood – I think he wrote a book or something. I thought I saw him a few minutes ago.' Perhaps it was more than she should have told him, but she suddenly felt very confused.

He seemed to think for a moment. 'Can't say I know a Michael Corrigan. There used to be a Master Corrigan, who taught school down near Tully, but I think he might be dead by now. No, if there were anybody else in this wood, I'd probably have seen them. I've been about since early morning and you're the first person I've seen.' A twig fell somewhere in the woodland behind him.

'I … I was just looking at that big stone over there....' Sinéad was desperately looking for something to say. Liam was standing so close to her that he could have put his arm around her. 'What is it? I think there's some writing on it.'

He followed her gaze and shrugged. 'Just a stone,' he said, 'overgrown with grass and weeds. I don't think there's any writing on it – maybe just cracks or something on its surface.'

'But Mr Corrigan told me there might be somebody buried in this wood – one of the old Hudsons that used to own these lands....' She was babbling. 'I thought this might be a … a headstone or something....'

Liam laughed loudly. In the gathering dark of the clearing, it sounded a little unpleasant, like the harsh, mocking cawing of a crow. 'I never heard of that. There's lots of old legends connected with this wood, most of 'em utter nonsense. But I didn't think there was somebody buried here. It isn't a graveyard.' There was condescension in his tone.

Sinéad smiled weakly. Maybe old Michael Corrigan had got it wrong or made the whole thing up. If that was the case, he had made her look very stupid.

'There *was* some kind of shooting lodge here,' Liam was saying. 'Built by the people that owned this wood. I've always thought this was a great place for a lodge – so open, so sunny.' His face clouded a little. 'Of course, there's nothing left of it now. But I'm sure it was a grand place in its day.'

'I … I'm sorry,' Sinéad murmured. 'I got it wrong. It's just that I was told –'

'Oh, there's a lot of stories about this place. They say that three little girls vanished here years ago. What they don't say was that those girls were in their teens, and that they probably ran off to Dublin or Cork. But, over the years, the stories have built up – got more and more strange and grotesque. There've been tales about ghosts, monsters, heaven knows what else, living in this wood. All I know is that I've never seen anything, and I've been here for …' He seemed to hesitate. '… I've been coming here for years.'

There was something odd about his words, his manner, that unsettled Sinéad. She wasn't sure whether she liked this Liam or not. He seemed overly dismissive of everything she'd been told. Besides, he was being very familiar towards her; he was now standing closer than seemed decent. And, despite his condescending attitude, she was almost sure that there were words on the stone, not just cracks.

'I … I should be getting back now. Is there a path out of here?' All she wanted to do was get away from the gloomy clearing, away from Liam and the weird overgrown stone, away from the sinister trees.

He laid a hand on her upper arm, an intimate gesture that startled her a little. 'Of course. I'll take you back to the edge of the wood. If you just come with me, there's a direct way out over here.' And he gently guided her towards the edge of the clearing, where another narrow path disappeared among the trees. Shadows seemed to spread across the clearing with increasing rapidity, sweeping over them both.

Sinéad remembered nothing of the way to the edge of the

wood, only vague impressions of interlocking tree-branches and clumps of foxgloves. Then there she was, on the very edge of Dungort, looking across the open fields towards the bungalows. Liam was still by her side, holding her upper arm.

'There you are. The edge of the wood at last! Quicker than you thought, too, I'd imagine.' He let go of her arm. 'Maybe I'll see you again before you go.'

Sinéad had expected him to come with her towards the bungalows, but he turned back towards the wood. 'I live on the other side,' he explained. As his hand fell away, she thought that it looked old and liver-spotted, like that of an elderly man. Yet his face was still young.

She nodded and turned away. Liam's smile was almost wolfish as she left him standing among the trees and turned to make her way back to the road. She suddenly felt very tired and weak, and there was an odd pain just behind her left ear, where the hairline came down. It felt as though somebody had hit her; but when she put her hand to it, she couldn't feel a lump. Maybe, she thought, she had been struck by a low-hanging branch – or it might be an insect bite of some sort; but she couldn't remember being either struck or bitten. It was very odd.

As she toiled over the uneven field, she chanced to look down at her watch. Almost four hours had passed since she'd left her aunt's house, and yet it had only felt like one or two. She'd probably missed the priest again. Her aunt would be furious.

But Aunt Barbara seemed pleased to see her. Once again, something was cooking on the range, and the old woman had obviously been waiting for Sinéad so that they could eat. Sinéad had never been in a place where so much was eaten; it must give Aunt Barbara something to do, she thought, but if she kept on at this rate she'd be the size of a house before she left Ireland. The radio blasted out its news through the kitchen:

'... *Sean Crossley, heading the investigation, has stated*

that a man is helping them with their enquiries. He also said that Gardaí were pursuing several leads within the Tallaght area....'

'I ... I'm sorry, Aunt Barbara. I was over by Dungort Wood and I stayed longer than I thought. I just don't know where the time went. Have I missed Father ... er ... McCarthy?'

A mild flash of irritation crossed Aunt Barbara's face, but her pleasant manner remained. 'He rang just after you'd gone and said that he wasn't able to come round. An old man up by Kilgoran is likely to die, and the Father had to go up and give him the last rites. He'll be here tomorrow morning.'

Sinéad nodded. 'I think you might be wrong about Liam Rogan. He doesn't live in those new bungalows at all. He said he lived over on the other side of the wood.'

Her aunt's brows knitted in puzzlement. 'Then it can't have been Liam Rogan. He had a bungalow built along the side of the road with the money that he got from oul' Mary's will. It wouldn't be Liam Cosgrove, would it – oul' Paddy's eldest boy? A big fair-haired fellow with a wee bit of a squint in his left eye? I know he's supposed to have bought land somewhere between here and Tully Cross.'

'No.' Sinéad shook her head. 'He didn't look like that at all. He looked ... At one time I thought he was far older than he actually was.'

Aunt Barbara looked at her strangely. 'Then I don't know who it might be.' She shrugged. 'Probably somebody working on one of the farms round about.' She hunted in a drawer for cutlery. 'But I wouldn't go anywhere near Dungort – it's a bad place, Sinéad, everyone says so.'

'Why?' Sinéad was curious, anxious to hear more, but the old woman only fussed about the table, laying places.

'They've caught somebody for the murder of that wee girl in Dublin,' she changed the subject. 'They say he knew her. He's "helping them with their enquiries", but they'll arrest him soon enough. Far too many of those sort of people about.

Especially around Dublin – I hear it's a bad place, full of sex and drugs. Nobody's safe there....' And her comments set the tone for the next couple of hours, as she raked up everything she'd heard about the badness of big cities – Dublin, London, New York – while Sinéad listened wearily. Her tiredness increased, grad-ually turning into an aching weariness, and she found herself nodding off even as her aunt spoke. She couldn't follow the conversation; she found herself grunting in inappropriate places. Finally, she admitted defeat and suggested that she should go to bed.

Aunt Barbara looked at her worriedly but agreed. 'Have a lie-in in the morning,' she suggested kindly. 'Before Father McCarthy comes.'

Sinéad nodded, excused herself, and went up to her bedroom. Falling on top of the narrow bed without even taking her clothes off, she was soon asleep.

⚜

The dream was particularly vivid. She was making her way along the narrow earthen path that twisted between the trees; she jumped across a small stream, ploughed through clusters of foxglove and laurel, and emerged in that same clearing. Light and shadows dappled the long grasses and tall nettles that waved their heads in welcome.

The large stone was still there, although it didn't seem so overgrown this time. Sinéad thought she could make out some words on it, incised very deeply, although as she watched they all seemed to run together in cracks. '... *HUDSO ... Died 18 ...*' She couldn't make out the rest.

'It *was* a burial ground!' she heard herself exclaim, the sound of her voice echoing off the wall of trees all around.

'Oh, indeed it was!' said a voice behind her. Turning, she saw Liam standing on the very edge of the clearing. There was something odd about him – the way the queer light played across his face, making him look first old, then young, then a mixture of the two. His hair seemed to change colour as the sun moved round the glade – now golden, now dark, now grey. The hand he extended towards her was first that of a young man, then spotted and marked like that of an elderly pensioner, then a claw. 'There are some very special people buried here.'

He was a young man once again, and Sinéad thought she had never seen anybody so attractive. He was walking towards her, across the intervening space; but, once again, he seemed to be changing. And there was a smell in the air – a nasty, corrupt stench, like rotting meat or overflowing drains – the stench of death and decay, although whether it came from Liam himself or from the ground around the stone, she didn't really know.

'It's yourself, Kitty,' he was saying. 'Just as I remember you. Come on and give me a kiss, the way you used to!'

Sinéad shrank back, but he was taking long, long steps towards her, covering the ground between them faster than seemed humanly possible.

'No!' she shouted. 'Stay away! For God's sake, stay away!'

'I've been waiting for you, Kitty.' The voice was persistent. 'Or for somebody like you.'

'Please!' she whimpered. 'Not me! It's not me you want.... Haven't I had enough misery in my life?'

Liam smiled, and his claw-hand touched her. She recoiled at the coldness of it. The awful stench grew stronger.

'Oh, no, Sinéad. Not nearly enough. I've waited too long for this moment to let it go.'

Sinéad woke in a sweat, with the morning sun streaming in through the still-drawn curtains. Her head pounded and she felt weak and sick. The pain behind her ear throbbed more than ever.

Pulling herself out from between the sweaty sheets, she swung her legs over the edge of the bed and almost lost her balance as she put her feet on the floor. The room seemed to spin around her, and she had to grip the bedside table to steady herself.

She managed to cross the room and pull the curtains wide. Away across the fields, Dungort Wood still waved, and the very sight of it made her stomach heave. Raising her fingertips to the back of her left ear, she felt a small lump; when she brought her hand away, there was blood on her fingers. She had banged herself in her sleep, she reasoned; that was the only explanation.

After washing and dressing, Sinéad went downstairs, where the smell of fried cooking made her stomach somersault and the customary sound of the radio assailed her senses.

'... *have charged a man with the murder of eight-year-old Mary O'Connor, whose body was found at a disused factory in Tallaght, Dublin, earlier this week. Although he has not been named, the man is said to have been a close friend of the O'Connor family....*'

'Didn't I tell you he'd be charged?' asked Aunt Barbara triumphantly, looking up from the frying-pan. Sinéad's stomach heaved – she didn't feel well at all. 'Didn't I tell you that there were far too many of those sort of people about Dublin?'

Sinéad nodded wanly.

'You're looking very peaky,' said her aunt, concerned. 'Did you have a bad night?'

Sinéad shook her head. 'I – I'll be all right,' she answered. 'Honestly.'

But, despite her assurances, she had no appetite for her breakfast. She pushed pieces of fried bread around her plate while Aunt Barbara looked on anxiously. Conversation between them came in fits and starts and was about nothing of significance. Father McCarthy's imminent visit was barely mentioned.

After breakfast, Sinéad announced that she was going to get some air. Behind Aunt Barbara's small two-storey house, a small, rather overgrown garden sloped away to a thick hedge

that separated it from the fields beyond; a peeling gate kept
out the grazing cows and sheep. The day was heavy, threatening
rain, but there was a hint of sunshine and the air was warm.
Sitting down on a creaky, lopsided garden seat, Sinéad soaked
up what early-morning sun she could, until Aunt Barbara put
her head out of the kitchen window and announced: 'Sinéad!
There's somebody here to see you!'

She expected it to be Father McCarthy, but it wasn't. It
was Michael Corrigan's sour-looking daughter. As Sinéad came
into the kitchen, the woman stared at her, her face almost as
thunderous as the weather outside.

'I didn't want to come see you,' she announced, without
any greeting. 'But Dada's been a bit ... restless lately. He's still
convinced that you're Bridie Burke, and nothing I can say'll
dissuade him. He believes that you're in some sort of danger,
and he's asked me to give you this.' She held out a little package,
nothing more than a small paper bag folded over on itself. 'I
tried to talk him out of it, but he's that bull-headed.... So I
promised I'd give it to you, an' you might as well take it.' And
she thrust the package into a startled Sinéad's hands, then,
turning quickly on her heel, walked out of the kitchen.

Aunt Barbara looked after her wonderingly. 'I don't know
how she puts up with that oul' man an' his notions,' she
whispered. 'He should be in a home. What's he sent you?'

Inquisitively Sinéad pulled away the wrapping. The bag
contained nothing but a yellowing magazine, with a small,
dark crucifix rammed between two of the pages like a
bookmark. She took the crucifix out and examined it; it seemed
to be made of some strange black wood with which she was
not familiar. The pages where it had been placed contained
nothing but several faded photographs. The magazine was some
sort of parish publication from the 1950s, but the pictures
reprinted in it were far older than that; there was no date on
any of them, but, judging by the clothes of the people in them,
they looked as though they might be from the late nineteenth
century.

And there was Liam, standing at the centre of a photograph taken on what was clearly the edge of Dungort Wood. He looked much older than he had when Sinéad had seen him, but there was no mistaking his features. Underneath were the words, 'William Hudson, taken near his hunting lodge.'

William – Liam – it all seemed to fit. The missing time in the wood ... the blood behind her ear ... the way he had shifted from old age to youth and back again.... Sinéad's blood turned cold, and she had the sensation that things were whispering in her ear. The room seemed to move of its own accord for a moment, then steady itself.

Sinéad caught her breath. It *couldn't* be the same man, surely! The stress of the past couple of years was catching up with her. Liam might be somehow related to the man in the picture, which would account for the resemblance. That *had* to be it. Either that, or she was losing her mind.

She read on. There was a little piece about William Hudson; even at a glance, it clearly made him out to be a bad landlord. It stopped short of making any of the allegations that old Michael Corrigan had hinted at, but Sinéad read between the lines. A reference to Hudson's strong connection with Dungort Wood; a mention of a girl – unnamed – who had disappeared near his hunting lodge many years before; a few words about his liking for blood sports....

To get away from the disconcerting photograph, she turned over the page, and found herself looking at a photograph of a stern-faced priest. The legend beside the picture read, 'Father Francis Fawley on his return from the African missions.'

'My God!' Aunt Barbara was looking at the magazine over Sinéad's shoulder. 'So that's Father Fawley. I've heard Father McCarthy speaking about him. He was a parish priest here, years ago, before he went to the missions. A very holy man, he was!' She almost genuflected before the picture.

The brief passage beside the photo bore this reputation out. Father Fawley had indeed been a very religious – and, according to the report, much loved – parish priest. He had gone off to the African missions, where he had served as a rural clergyman and as an exorcist. He was still 'much thought of', and had returned to Ireland to a warm welcome in his former parish. Looking at the photo of the tall, austere man, Sinéad noticed that, hanging against the front of his cassock, was the very crucifix she now held in her hand. The cross of an exorcist! She seemed to sense power emanating from it, and she closed her hand tightly around it.

'I used to hear about Father Fawley,' Aunt Barbara was saying. 'About how holy he was. A very sacred and sincere man. They used to say that no evil thing could even come near him. That crucifix in the picture looks like the one you're holding in your hand, Sinéad.'

Indeed, it did – it was the same. Sinéad handed the magazine to her aunt, who skimmed through it in wonder, and wandered out of the kitchen towards the back of the house. She suddenly felt very ill.

'I'm away out to the garden. I'm not feeling the best at all, Aunt Barbara.' But her aunt was lost in the old black-and-white photos and didn't reply.

Away across the field, the wood seemed to be waiting. Sinéad went down to the foot of the garden and leaned on the gate, looking across at the gently waving trees. Almost without thinking, and with no conscious volition, she slipped the latch and went out into the field, towards the wood. She felt herself being drawn to the dark depths of Dungort, as if someone – or something – was calling to her. In her hand, she clutched the tiny crucifix so tightly that it almost hurt.

The spaces between the trees seemed darker than ever, and peculiar shadows darted here and there. Tentatively Sinéad stepped into the shade at the edge of the wood. She was unsure why she'd come – it was as though something unseen called her into the dark undergrowth. She brushed away a low-hanging branch and negotiated a clump of laurel to venture deeper into the gloom.

Tiny half-lit trails led away into the wood, branches shadowing them like cathedral roofs. She stepped along one, feeling the mossy mulch give under her feet. Here and there an old tree-stump, green with moss, rose up out of the woodland floor, and several times she almost stumbled in the twilit gloom. Away at the end of the track she could see a vague, smoky light that suggested open air, and she made her way towards it. The trees clustered around her oppressively, letting little light through their branches. There seemed to be faint and furtive whisperings everywhere.

Sinéad gripped the crucifix until she could feel it dig into her palm, drawing a bead of blood. Looking upwards, she couldn't even see the sky, only the dark interlocking branches of the trees; the air along the track was so cold that she felt she was in a tomb. Snatches of her dream drifted back to her and she shivered, not only from the chill. In the near-dark she stubbed her foot against a branch, half-hidden in the mulch, and found herself hobbling the last yards towards the light.

Tall ferns and nettles waved at her as she emerged from the tiny track and onto a wider pathway, which led down a brief decline and into a clearing. As she stepped out from between the trees, she recognised the familiar stone and the clumps of foxgloves nearby. This was the place where she had last met Liam – the clearing that must lie at the very heart of Dungort Wood. The place seemed filled with a writhing, smoky sunlight, and the whispering from amongst the surrounding foliage increased. It was as though a muttering throng had gathered to watch her as she came out into the open.

He was waiting for her near the large stone. Where he had come from, Sinéad was not altogether sure; one moment she was alone, and the next Liam was with her. She had the distinct impression of some kind of a building close by, although she could see nothing; it seemed that he had just opened a door and walked through to greet her.

'I knew you'd come,' he said softly, his voice rising only

slightly above the continual murmuring from the trees around him. 'I've been waiting here to see you again, and I knew you'd come back to Dungort if I called you.'

The impression of a dwelling somewhere behind him grew stronger; Sinéad could almost see the outlines of a lodge of some sort – the doors, the windows.... And, at one of the windows, three wan, bloodless faces stared back at her. Girls in their teens, so pale that they were almost blue, their lips moving soundlessly. They were clearly not of her world but of some terrible Otherworld that lay beyond the wood, beyond her understanding.

This is what he wants for me, her mind told her. *These are the three girls who vanished – they never left this wood – and I'm to be the fourth.*

'*He waits for the hurt, the fearful, the lonely....*' Old Michael Corrigan's words sounded somewhere in her memory. Liam was advancing on her, his hand outstretched in greeting. Father Fawley's crucifix dug so deeply into the flesh of her hand that she could feel the blood trickling down her wrist.

Aloud she said, 'You're William Hudson, aren't you?' Her voice seemed strangely distorted in the glade, and the whispering in the wood seemed to grow more frantic at the sound of it.

He gave a small, grave bow of acknowledgement. 'You're frightened of me – don't be. My people have owned these woodlands for centuries, but they never fully understood what they had. These were pagan lands; old spirits have dwelt among these trees since the beginning of time. I was able to harness their energies – become their embodiment and, in a strange way, gain a sort of immortality. As in the time of the old Celtic people, the gods of this wood took on form and substance in me, and I've lived here ever since.

'I was killed and buried here – no church would have my body – and yet I didn't die as you understand it. I lived on here, in the wood, making sure that all paths through Dungort led to me. The wood-spirits protected me, granted me life eternal, and only demanded a sacrifice of blood once in a while. And, as I was their embodiment, *I* took the blood – the blood of foolish, lonely girls. And through them I lived on – and they lived on through me. Just as you will, Sinéad. Now come to me, for we've talked enough and the spirits of this place are very hungry.'

He was almost touching her now, and she felt her pulse quicken. 'We can live together in this wood forever, away from the outside world. Away from the prying of foolish people, away from peeping priests and their like....' His outstretched hand seemed positively reassuring.

'Himself is always about, waitin' for the likes of you....' Old Michael Corrigan's voice echoed warningly somewhere in the back of Sinéad's mind, and for a fleeting moment she had the impression of a huge, bloated, obscene spider in the centre of its web – the wood – drawing vulnerable women to it. She pushed the notion away.

'That's it!' whispered Liam, as if he could read her mind. 'Forget about the everyday world. Take my hand.'

Slowly Sinéad held out her right hand, and for a second they touched. Liam's fingers touched Father Fawley's crucifix, which seemed embedded in her flesh.

He screamed, a long, haunting sound, like the cry of a horn deep in the wood. It seemed to be echoed from everywhere around. Momentarily, the strange lodge seemed to gain solidity – Sinéad saw the open door and the faces of the girls at the window, each mouth opened in a repetition of Liam's own scream. Then it was gone and there was only Liam, directly in front of her, his whole body jerking as if in a spasm. The cold wind sprang up and whistled between the trees, chilling her to the bone.

'That ... that *thing*!' he hissed. 'Take it away!'

'... *the hurt, the fearful, the lonely....*' The distant voice rang in her ears. Then Aunt Barbara's: '... *a saintly man. Very holy....*'

'... *Betrayed*!' Liam fell backwards, leaning on the great stone, and then was gone. With a sound like thunder, the stone itself cracked along the fissure lines and fell apart. Sinéad was alone in the clearing, fragments of broken stone lying at her feet. The crucifix fell from her hand, covered with her blood, and was lost amongst the tall grasses and foxgloves.

She shook her head, as though emerging from some dream. The quality of the light in the glade seemed to have changed subtly. No more was it a dull, smoky, threatening brilliance; it had become a more healthy, friendly illumination. The wind had dropped and the clearing was very still. Of Father Fawley's crucifix, there was no sign.

Cautiously, Sinéad took a few steps towards the edge of the nearby trees.

As she walked back towards the edge of Dungort Wood, Sinéad realised that the oppressiveness of the place seemed to have lifted. Although the trees and the pathside bushes still stood in the same places, there seemed to be more space between them; and, while there was still darkness along the little trails that ran off into the foliage, somehow they didn't seem quite so menacing.

Father McCarthy would be waiting for her at her aunt's house, and somehow she was no longer afraid of him. Even as she watched, a small bird lit on a nearby branch and began to ease its throat in song. The way through the wood seemed easier now, and Sinéad quickened her pace to get home.

THE WITHERED HAND

'Let me show you something, Daniel,' exclaimed Farrant, his eyes wide and almost feverish with excitement. 'I guarantee you'll not have seen anything like it before. It's totally unique – you've my word for that.' And for Richard Farrant that was something of a grand claim, for he was a collector of the unusual, the bizarre and the downright grotesque.

Outside, a dank and dismal day was steadily fading around Innocent House – if ever a place was totally misnamed, it had to be this one – and a stealthy, smoky darkness crept across the Fens beyond the window where we stood. A late bird called somewhere in the encroaching marsh that met the overgrown grounds of Farrant's home.

I had known Richard Farrant since we were at school together – in fact, we both came from the same village in Essex. I was the son of a local schoolmaster, while Farrant's father 'did something' up in London. I don't know what originally drew the two of us together; maybe it was a shared interest in things historical. Even as a young man, I remember, Farrant had been a bit *unusual* – a dreamy, disconnected individual, unable to settle. When we both went to university, he'd been exactly the same. He was brilliant enough, and he could probably have achieved a great many things – as a teacher, a lecturer, a leading researcher – but his temperament had always let him down. He seemed unable to apply himself to anything for any length of time – anything except his daydreams and curious interests. Formal history bored him, and he found studying something of a chore. And I suppose the relative laxness of university life allowed him to develop the more bizarre side of his nature.

As far as I can make out, he became much worse after visiting a run-down bookshop in Exeter, owned (he said) by a witch-like old woman and a black cat. Here he bought a mildewed copy of Paul Klinn's *A Journey to the Far Mountains*. Those of you who don't know the history of this particular work may imagine it to be some sort of comfortable travelogue, but I can assure you that it's certainly not! Supposedly written around the end of the nineteenth century by a Dutchman styling himself 'Paul Klinn', it claims to be an account of his travels to 'the unknown lands of Araby and the Oriental countries' in search of the unusual and the occult. It describes, in ghoulish detail, certain rites carried out by 'the Aetheop peoples' and in 'the unvisited monasteries of the high Himalayas', as well as outlining 'many curious spells and much demonological lore of a medieval antiquity'. Whether this book is even remotely accurate, or nothing more than concocted mumbo-jumbo, has long been debated amongst scholars and occultists. There have even been strong suggestions that 'Klinn' himself never existed and that the whole thing was an elaborate hoax to deceive the gullible; and yet, the descriptions of certain locations are reputedly accurate. The book would probably have gone unremarked had it not attracted the interest of Aleister Crowley sometime around 1914; the self-styled 'Great Beast' pronounced it to be 'a work of monumental importance' and instantly made it a cult classic amongst would-be demonologists. There were several English reprints of the tome; the most easily available was published in London in 1937 by Nahum and Son (who appear to have gone out of business soon afterward). It was a badly stained, dog-eared copy of this edition that Farrant picked up in the Exeter bookshop.

The book had an electrifying effect on him. It jerked him out of his torpor and gave him purpose and drive – albeit not in altogether wholesome directions. In his *Journey,* 'Paul Klinn' makes reference to many ancient and fabulous books, and some of these – the more esoteric the better, it seemed – Richard Farrant seemed absolutely driven to hunt out.

Throughout his undergraduate days, he ignored his studies in order to track down half-mythological manuscripts such as Robert Flud's *Chiromancy*, de Stampa's *Satanae,* the *Teufelbuchen* of that crazed old Johannes Ruchlinn, and Mannering's *Discourses on the Arts of Witchcraft* – literature that no sane scholar should read. He sought this material from libraries all over the country, through university channels, under the guise of 'research'. The majority of the books were, of course, unavailable, or else kept under lock and key and released only to those with the most scrupulous references – which Richard Farrant didn't have. And, as time passed, his tastes became much weirder. I remember how he pestered the staff at the university library for months, trying to get them to hunt down a particularly obscure volume that they had really no chance of obtaining for him – the *Vigiliae Mortuorum Secundum Chorum Ecclesiae Maguntinae,* a manual of ritual from a long-forgotten and greatly abhorred church – before giving up in disgust. At the time, Farrant didn't have the finances to undertake such a quest for himself. That, however, was soon to change.

I had never really met Farrant's parents, apart from brief hellos at social occasions, but I knew that his father had done reasonably well in London. Richard was their only child and they spoiled him, indulging his idleness and strange tastes with a patience known only to the most devoted parents. They died within weeks of each other, leaving him some property (which he quickly sold) and a tidy sum in the bank. Although he wasn't overly wealthy, he now had enough money to indulge some of his more *outré* passions.

He sold his parents' house and bought a large, rambling place in the Fen country – a property known as Innocent House. It probably appealed to Farrant, firstly, because of its remoteness, and secondly, because an ancient and particularly brutal murder had taken place there, leaving the building with a reputation for being haunted. I knew that the property was in a fairly dilapidated state – presumably this also appealed to him. He dropped out of university completely and went to live in his newly acquired residence.

I say he went to 'live' there, but he seemed to inhabit the place only infrequently, spending most of his time up in London. Speculation was rife that he was frittering away his parents' money on shows and clubs, but I imagined that most of it finished up in the hands of 'specialist' booksellers in the back streets of the city, who could indulge his taste for bizarre and occult literature. I later learned that I was right: each time Farrant returned to Innocent House from the city, he was carrying masses of books that he would let no one else see. It seemed evident that he was building up some kind of awful, arcane library for himself in the depths of his new property. That was the last that I heard of Farrant for a while, for I then lost contact with him for several years.

Our reunion happened completely by accident. On one of my infrequent trips into London, I'd stopped into a café to grab a sandwich before catching the train home; and there he was. I didn't even recognise him, so unkempt and gaunt had he become; the clothes hung on his awkward, stick-like frame as on a tattered scarecrow.

Farrant recognised me instantly, although I now wish to God that he hadn't. As I stood at the till, he caught my arm with an eager ferocity. 'Daniel! Daniel Curtis! Well, well, this is amazing. I was just thinking about you, and there you are.'

I think he expected me to know who he was right away (which, of course, I didn't – much to his disappointment). I had to think for a moment before his name clicked into place. He had changed greatly – he looked even wilder than I remembered from university. His face seemed a great deal older, and there was a kind of queer *unwholesomeness* about him –

a sly furtiveness that, initially at least, made me a bit uneasy in his company. I thought, too, that he looked distinctly unwell, pale and peaky, with great dark shadows under his eyes. On his neck, I noticed a great, livid scar or weal, which I couldn't remember from our university days; I wondered about it but didn't mention it, and nor did he. His manner was peculiar, too: he vacillated between long bursts of nervous energy and periods of near-lethargy. In fact, most of the time he seemed to be running on adrenaline alone.

He greeted me as if we'd never been apart, recalling long-forgotten conversations almost word for word, as if they'd only happened the day before, and launching into long and disconnected monologues about life in the Fens. It was a bizarre conversation; Farrant continually went off at tangents, his sentences running together in a most disconcerting way. And under all his frantic talk bubbled a hysterical, barely suppressed excitement.

From what I could gather, he'd done little or nothing with his life since dropping out of university – nothing concrete, that is. He'd been 'reading, researching and collecting'. He was (as he told me excitedly) working on an academic paper, which would 'revolutionise man's thinking about his relationship with the supernatural and with organised religion', but it was taking longer than he'd anticipated. I was surprised to learn that he'd been following my post-university career with an interest that almost bordered on obsession – we'd certainly been good friends as undergraduates, but we'd never really been *that* close. In particular, he'd been collating a number of articles I'd written on primitive religions, which he found 'stimulating' and especially relevant to his own work.

'We simply *must* remain in contact,' he insisted. Foolishly, I agreed and gave him my home telephone number, hoping that after a few scattered exchanges he'd lose interest in talking to me.

For the next few weeks, I was literally bombarded with

calls. Farrant always called me at unusual hours – sometimes early in the morning, when he 'did his best thinking' but when more conventional people were still in bed – to discuss some point of religious philosophy. He would talk for hours. I began to dread his calls – I let the answering machine take a couple of them, which I never returned – and yet there was *something* in his line of research that interested me to the point of fascination.

I gathered that he had squandered most of his inheritance on very obscure books. He trafficked with 'dealers', most of whom I suspected were of the shadiest kind, whose only purpose was to separate him from his money. They obtained for him (probably by criminal means) books that were hard to locate. Certainly no university that I knew of held even a few of the volumes he claimed to have in his unholy 'library'. He mentioned, for instance, *The Mysteries of Yig* – which is virtually unheard of in the West – and the *Directorium Inquisitorium*, written late in the fifteenth century by Eymeric de Guironne, a mad Dominican friar and allegedly a senior officer of the dreaded Holy Inquisition. These, and many more, Farrant claimed to have in his possession; and, despite my unease about the man, I would have given almost anything to see even one of them.

But there was more. He claimed to have obtained a number of bizarre *things* from some less-than-scrupulous dealers in antiquities. As if to whet my appetite, he mentioned a set of scrolls somehow connected to the infamous Black Crusade of the twelfth century; the blasphemous gold covering of Guido of Tiek's *Deathbook*, illuminated with ghastly part-human deities; a poisoned ring that had belonged to the fifteenth-century pirate anti-Pope 'John XXIII'…. Having an interest in the bizarre and unusual myself, I desperately wanted to see these artefacts, but I was hesitant to accept Farrant's repeated invitations to come down to the Fen Country for a weekend.

Finally, however, my curiosity got the better of me. One

evening, when Farrant rang me with his usual invitation, I told him that I could come down to Innocent House the following weekend. The prospect seemed to delight him beyond measure.

Innocent House, situated as it was on the very edge of a marsh, could never have been a wholly pleasant place to live. The house itself was architecturally pleasing, and its grounds seemed more than adequate; but the atmosphere of the nearby bog seemed to hang over it like a dreadful miasma, instantly killing any pleasantness the setting might have generated. It seemed to have penetrated even into the interior of the house, settling on everything like a faint but noxious mist. There was a certain oppressiveness about the place that made me wish I could simply view the promised curios and be on my way again.

This claustrophobic impression was not improved by the clutter – Farrant described it as either 'reference material' or 'work in progress' – that infested all the downstairs rooms. Innocent House was really little more than an extended farm-house – plenty of tiny, awkward rooms and corners, but not much space – and this accentuated Farrant's untidiness. Books were piled here and there; sheets of paper, some carrying only a few lines of writing, were crumpled underfoot; in the corner lay the remnants of several half-finished meals on cracked plates. What help he had originally employed about the house, he explained, had been paid off as his money went on more exotic books and collectibles. Lately he'd been forced to fend for himself, although he claimed to be 'comfortable enough', an opinion with which I did not exactly agree.

As a welcoming meal he served me what he called a stew, although my stomach had doubts that it was food of any sort and threatened to rise in revolt. We ate from rather dirty plates (a fact which didn't seem to bother Farrant), and before I could sit down I had to clear away piles of yellowing magazines and the inevitable loose sheets of paper.

Farrant talked animatedly, non-stop. He had nearly completed his 'paper', and he wanted me to have a look at it and discuss its implications with him – if I was prepared to stay for a few days. Grudgingly, I agreed. In return, he promised to show me some of his treasures, including a 'special' one that he had recently acquired.

'It came from Ireland,' he said eagerly, taking another mouthful of the slop he'd served us up. 'I've had it for a few months now, and I've been dying to show it to somebody. It's a real find, and the way I came by it was very curious.'

He was clearly anxious to tell me about the curio, so I motioned him to go ahead.

'It's the hand of Lady Killigrew,' he announced grandly, as if I should know exactly what he was talking about. I looked at him blankly. 'You *must* have heard of the Killigrews of Bantry – they were great landholders in Cork around the time of the Plantation of Munster. Sir James Killigrew was created Warden of West Cork by Elizabeth I herself, way back in the late 1500s, but the family had already been in Cork for generations. Nobody seems to know where they came from or how they got their money, but it was said that they were what was left of an old Norman family who'd been in Ireland since the days of Strongbow, and that they were heavily involved in piracy and smuggling all along the Cork coast.'

Farrant's eyes were alive with the old excitement that I remembered from our undergraduate days. 'And there were plenty of really colourful characters among them. Sir Robert Killigrew, for instance: he was said to have married a woman from the sea – a mermaid – and sired a line of queer, half-human creatures who were kept well out of sight. Then there were Thomas Killigrew – a wild, violent man, who was said to drink the blood of his enemies – and his brother John, who allegedly plundered shipping as far away as the Scottish Isles.' He paused, still obviously excited. 'Quite a stream of strange and infamous characters. But the worst of them all was a woman – although she wasn't really of true Killigrew blood at all.'

I confessed that I'd never heard of her, nor of the family.

'Lady Alice Killigrew. Some accounts say that she was married to Sir James, the first Warden of West Cork; others say she was his mother, the wife of Desmond, who was the first of the line to be knighted by the English. Anyway, she lived around the 1580s, and she was feared throughout Ireland. She was a kind of pirate queen in West Cork, and many said she was a witch as well!'

'And you've got her *hand*?' I asked incredulously.

Farrant nodded eagerly. 'Her right hand. Struck off to prevent her from working magic, just before they hanged her. Maybe they thought she would try to save herself from the gallows or something. All the stories about her say that she could kill a man with one wave of her hand. That's why they cut it off – and, according to folklore, the wound didn't bleed, because she wasn't really human. The hand was presumed lost, but I have it upstairs in my study! Do you want to see it? I can show it to you now!'

He was as eager as a schoolboy, but I shook my head. I was tired after my journey; and, truthfully, the 'meal' had left me with a queasy feeling that wasn't helped by Farrant's chatter. I just wanted to stretch out somewhere, well away from his continual questioning.

'Maybe tomorrow,' I replied. 'I really need a rest after the journey.'

Farrant seemed vastly disappointed, like a child that has been scolded. I tried to reassure him of my interest.

'You said you'd come by it in a peculiar way?'

His mood lifted again; the fevered light returned to his eyes, and he took a sup of his awful gruel with renewed enthusiasm.

'Yes. I came home one evening to find old Garret, one of my suppliers, waiting for me just outside the gate. He had a small brown cardboard box under his arm. I was really puzzled to see him here; he'd travelled up from London just to see me – something he wouldn't normally do for his clients. Anyway, I brought him in, and he didn't seem to be at ease at all – there was something very nervy about him. At first I thought it had something to do with me, but later I decided it had to do with the box under his arm. From time to time, I thought I heard a faint scratching sound, like a mouse gnawing to get out; but it was more an impression than a real sound, and it was gone as soon as I'd sensed it.

"'I've brought you something special, Mr Farrant," he said in that sly way of his. "Something you won't find anywhere else." He's a furtive, greasy man with long hanks of dirty hair and a narrow, ferrety face. He keeps a grubby little shop in a back lane in Whitechapel, where he sells oddments and one or two books of – ah – dubious antiquity. I don't like dealing with him at all, but he can sometimes get me some interesting volumes, and – er – other things as well. I suspected that it was one of those other things that had brought him down from London.

"'Well, Mr Garret," I asked, "what is this rare prize?"

'He set the box down on the table and slid the lid back a little, as if he were trying to tease me. The more I looked at him, the more repulsive he seemed. Yet there was a certain – uneasiness – about him, as if he wanted to sell me this "special" item and be gone. Mistakenly, I thought he might be frightened of Innocent House itself – it has a reputation for being haunted, you know.

"'It's a hand, Mr Farrant," he said, "but no ordinary hand, I can tell you. It's the hand of Lady Alice Killigrew of Bantry!"

'He didn't have to explain any more; I knew all about Lady Alice. He opened the box a little further, and I glimpsed the hand inside it. I noticed, too, that his own hand seemed to be trembling a bit as he slid back the lid.

"'Do you want to see more?" he asked, in that furtive, unpleasant way of his.

'I nodded. He drew back the lid fully, and I saw the hand myself for the first time. Maybe it was the poor light in the room, but I honestly thought at the time that it *moved* a little as I fixed my eyes on it. I looked again, and it was perfectly still.'

I treated this with suspicion; Farrant was prone to a little shameless exaggeration when the mood took him.

'Maybe it was the way the old man's hand trembled. He was clearly very uncomfortable with the thing.

'"Is it authentic?" I asked him, even though I knew this was a foolish question. The other things I had bought from Garret had been completely genuine, and I knew better than to ask him where he'd obtained them; Garret mostly traded in goods that had been "appropriated", so to speak. He was clearly anxious to get rid of this one. Maybe I could use this eagerness to my advantage, I thought.

'"Oh, it's genuine all right, Mr Farrant!" he replied. "If you know anything at all about the old Lady, you'll know that the second finger of her right hand was cut off at the tip. Some people say it was done in a fight with the English when they came to arrest her; others will tell you it was done somewhere else. And she had a queer mark – a birthmark or something – just at the base of her thumb. But look for yourself, sir. Seeing's believing." And he pointed to the shrivelled hand in the box. The tip of the second finger was certainly missing; and against the withered skin at the base of the thumb, there was indeed a dark mark that vaguely resembled a star.

'"Now, I have to get back to London, and there's a train I can't afford to miss. Do you want this or not? I can give it to you for a knockdown price, seein' as how you're one of my regulars." He made me sound like some sort of pervert doing business with a prostitute. One of his "regulars", indeed!

'But I *was* intrigued by the hand. If what Garret told me was even half-true, then this was a truly rare item. The very hand a witch had used to work her terrible spells! What an addition to my collection!

'"It depends on how much you're asking for it," I replied.

'Garret knew he had me, so he named an outrageous figure. He was scared of the hand, that was clear, but apparently he was determined to make some sort of profit on it. I dismissed the sum, expecting him to haggle; but, to my astonishment, he dropped the price so low that I couldn't believe it. He had only been chancing his arm; he was almost ready to *give* away the hand in order to get it out of his possession. Hence the journey from London.

'I couldn't pass it up; and that's how the thing became mine. Odd, don't you think?'

'Very,' I replied. 'I can't wait to see it. But first – bed, if you'll show me where you want me to sleep.'

Even though Farrant still seemed reluctant, this more or less brought our evening to an end.

The room Farrant gave me was a peculiar one, in what was obviously the oldest part of the building. Innocent House, he had told me, had originally been nothing more than a large estate house, but successive families had added wings and annexes. Where the name had come from, Farrant was unsure – it might have had something to do with a previous occupant. My room was queerly constructed, with a sloping ceiling that created odd nooks and corners. It boasted a large fireplace – too large for the room, I thought – and a narrow window that hardly admitted enough light to see by; when the light outside was poor, the room was practically in darkness. It was partly panelled with heavy, dark wood, which gave it an air of gloom that seemed to pervade even its meagre furniture – a bed, a small washstand and cupboard, a couple of chairs, and a small bookcase with a few mouldering books in it. A closer inspection, by the weak light of a bare bulb, revealed great patches of damp on the unpanelled portions of the walls and woodworm in the bookcase. The door was an awkward, heavy thing that hung uncertainly on rusting hinges; the lock was broken and seemed to have been so for some time, and, though I tried, I couldn't get it to shut tightly. Not a cheery room, by any means; but then, I didn't intend to stay in it for very long. I found it very narrow and confined – since a child, I've suffered from a kind of claustrophobia – and I thought its walls pressed in on me, echoing the oppression of the whole house and of the marsh beyond.

It was a cold room and I suspected a fire hadn't been lit in it for a long, long time, so I was anxious to get into bed – rickety though it was – and, I hoped, out of the chill. Before turning in, however, I automatically glanced at some of the crumbling volumes in the bookcase – I suppose it was the academic in me coming out – but found nothing of interest. Judging by the subject matter, they didn't even seem to belong to Farrant; maybe he'd inherited them when he bought the house. There were a couple of old German travel books on England, an illustrated book on insect life in the Fens, three scientific treatises, and an old volume of fairy stories illustrated by black-and-white woodcut-type illustrations.

I opened this last book, absently looking at the pictures, which seemed to have been drawn with painstaking precision. Some of the pages were torn, others badly stained with un-known substances, and the whole volume smelt of must and dirt. The stories were the usual children's tales – 'Jack and the Beanstalk', 'Little Red Riding Hood', 'The Brave Tailor' – and were written in old-fashioned, formal English.

But it was the drawings that caught my eye. They were truly horrible, owing more to the diseased imagination of the artist than to the content of the tales. Here were witches who looked barely human, deformed and monstrous giants, dwarves that looked more like demons from the pit of hell. One drawing in particular caught my eye. It illustrated the story of 'Hansel and Gretel' and showed a barely human witch-woman hanging over the half-door of a tumbledown cottage. In one corner of the picture, the wide-eyed Hansel and Gretel looked fearfully out of their hiding-place. Underneath the sketch, a couplet had been added in dark, heavy Gothic script:

> *Nibble, nibble, little mouse,*
> *Who is gnawing at my house?*

It was a reference, I suppose, to the gingerbread house that the witch tempted the children to eat. Although all the illustrations were grotesque, there was something about this particular one that sent a shiver down my spine. I found my hand trembling as I closed the book and put it back on the shelf.

As I had expected, the bed was chilly and damp, but at least I could stretch full-length upon it. Without undressing, I switched off the light and climbed in, feeling the bedsprings sag under me. The darkness of Innocent House swept over me like a shroud as I tried to relax. Slowly, I became aware of the sounds of an old house at night – the sighs and creaks of a building settling. I heard Farrant cough, away in the distance; the ticking of a clock at the end of the passage outside my room; the whisper of the wind in the empty chimney. There were other sounds, too – scratching and scurryings, like mice behind the panelling. Gradually I began to drift into a kind of half-sleep, in which I was vaguely aware both of flitting dreams and of what was happening in the room around me.

I don't know what time it was when someone tried the handle of my door. As I've said, the door wouldn't lock, but it was heavy and difficult to open; I'd noticed that the handle was very stiff. Lying in the utter dark, I heard someone push against the upper part of the door, then the squeak of the handle being turned as somebody tried to inch it open.

It could only be Farrant. I sat up in bed, banging the back of my head on the low headboard.

'Who's there? Richard?' I asked groggily.

There was no answer, but the sound of the turning door-handle suddenly ceased.

'Hello?'

There was silence for a moment; then the sound began again, slow and deliberate, as though someone was putting the full weight of his hand on the stiff handle in an attempt to force it to turn. I thought I heard another sound, too: a faint scratching, like the claws of a mouse, or like someone outside drawing a nail across the varnished woodwork of the door. The mice in the panelling became agitated, frisking and scampering with even greater frenzy. Again and again, as I lay there in the dark, someone tried to turn the stiff handle, seemingly without success.

'Richard?' I shouted again. 'Farrant! In God's name, what are you doing?'

The sounds stopped and a silence, more sinister than any noise, fell upon the room. For several minutes there was quiet; gradually the rustling of the mice died down. It was as if somebody had tried the door and, finding no way in, had passed on down the corridor.

Then the whole house echoed with a cry that I knew to be Farrant's voice. I sincerely pray that I never hear another cry like it. There was no doubt that it came from a human throat, but it was so terror-filled as to be frightening in its own right. It was somewhere between a shriek of fear and a cry of utter despair.

I leapt from my bed and snapped on the light. This time the door-handle turned easily enough, and I dashed down the passageway to Farrant's room.

'Richard?' I hammered on his door. 'Richard? Are you all right, man?'

There was a minute's silence inside the room; then the door, as heavy as my own, opened a fraction, and Farrant looked out. He was deathly pale, and his eyes were wide and staring. He looked terrified.

'Yes! Yes!' He sounded almost irritable. 'I'm all right – just a bit of a nightmare – there's nothing the matter. Go back to bed!'

'But that cry –' I began.

He made a dismissive motion. 'A nightmare, I said. Nothing to worry about. Some of my reading….' He didn't bother to finish the sentence. The door closed again, leaving me standing in the passage in an extremely puzzled and agitated state.

I went back to my own room, but I didn't sleep at all. My nerves were on edge, and every creak and whisper in the ancient building made me start up, expecting to see something. But there was nothing more for the rest of the night.

In the morning, Farrant looked as though he hadn't slept. He was exceptionally pale and there were large, dark shadows under his eyes. If I didn't know better, I'd have said that he'd been drinking heavily the night before and was suffering for it now. He never mentioned his cry, and nor did I. For some reason, the weal on his neck seemed bigger and more inflamed, but neither of us mentioned that either. Despite Farrant's obvious enthusiasm for my work, I was beginning to notice a distance developing between us. To tell the truth, I was not in great shape myself – a night without sleep had seen to that, and the slop and burnt toast that Farrant served for breakfast didn't help – but at least I could attempt a conversation, which was more than he seemed able to do.

However, as the day went on, he appeared to brighten slightly, and gradually he regained some of his old manner. I waited for the promised artefacts to appear, but they didn't. Instead, Farrant wanted to discuss his 'grand paper'. He even showed me several disjointed pages of it – little more than incoherent jottings, which I have to say made very little sense to me. After an hour of discussing obscure Oriental philosophies in my rather fragile state, I was ready for a break.

'You promised to show me the hand of Lady Killigrew,' I reminded Farrant. Was it my imagination, or did his eyes become more fevered at the mere mention of the loathsome thing?

'Yes, yes,' he murmured. 'I've wanted you to see it, Daniel.

Come on!' And, rising from his seat, he hurried from the room, with me following in his wake.

We climbed the awkward staircase and crossed a gloomy landing to a low door. Opening the door, Farrant ushered me into a shadowy, windowless study, strewn, of course, with books and loose sheets of paper. By the glare of a bare light-bulb, he hunted in the drawer of a sagging desk and emerged with a small, plain cardboard box. He paused for a moment, then suddenly opened it like a stage magician, revealing several layers of white tissue paper. He fumbled through them, with all the excitement of a small boy exploring a birthday present.

In the centre of the tissue paper lay a small, shrivelled brown thing that, at first glance, looked for all the world like a large lump of ordure. On closer inspection, however, I realised that it was indeed a hand. It was certainly shrunken and withered, but I could make out the general shape, and the long, long fingernails that seemed to take up most of the box. Despite the withered condition of the hand itself, the nails still seemed strong and appeared to have been heavily lacquered. A couple of them were slightly chipped and broken, but apart from that, they seemed in reasonably good condition. I noticed, too, that the second finger certainly did appear to be a little shorter than the others – part of its nail was missing – and that on the lower part of the thumb was a curious mark shaped like a star. I thought I had seen a similar sign before, in a book on the ancient and vanished land of Bho – a sign of great antiquity, symbolising obscene evil – but I couldn't be certain.

'There you are!' Farrant exclaimed triumphantly. 'The right hand of Lady Alice Killigrew of Bantry!'

I looked at it carefully. It didn't look like anything special – just a wizened, desiccated piece of dead flesh wrapped up in tissue paper.

'You said you don't know the full story of Lady Alice?' he went on. 'And I've only told you a fraction. I read it in an old book of Irish folktales, and since the hand's come into my possession I've read it again and again till I can almost remember it word for word. But you've never heard of her at *all*?' He sounded so incredulous that I began to feel ashamed of my ignorance.

Farrant half-closed his eyes and began to speak as though he were reciting:

'As I've said, the Killigrews of Bantry were a roguish crew – pirates and smugglers, most of them. Old records show that they held the lands around Kilmore and that they built Drumlane Abbey – a great, draughty barn of a place, set on the site of an old monastery on the cliffs overlooking the sea – for themselves. They swore loyalty to the English crown, but it's said that Sir Desmond Killigrew also dealt with the Spanish, who were England's enemies during the sixteenth century, when the mood took him. Spanish treasure often seemed to find its way into the Killigrews' coffers, and Killigrew women were often seen wearing clothes and jewellery that might have been plundered from some honest merchantman along the Irish coast.

'Now old Sir Desmond was certainly bad, but his son, Sir James, was worse. The pair of them, it was said, sat up in that great barn of a place like birds of prey, plotting and scheming how to plunder even further along the coastline. In an attempt to make a deal with them, the English made Sir James Warden of West Cork, but it made little difference. Their raids continued, ranging as far as the Western Isles of Scotland.

'Nobody is sure whose wife Lady Alice was – Sir Desmond's or Sir James's – or what her maiden name had been, or who her parents were or where she came from. Let's say that she was married to Sir James for the sake of the story that I'm going to tell you.

'One evening, Sir James was out hunting on Kilworth Moor, which is a wild and lonely place in the north of Cork. Somewhere near the village of Kilmurry, a strange mist came down on the party and Sir James Killigrew got separated from the others. He rode on through unknown country, becoming more and more lost as the fog grew thicker and thicker. Then, somewhere on the moor, the mist suddenly cleared and he found himself looking down into a narrow valley.

'This is where all the stories differ. Some versions say he saw an abandoned house down there; others say it was only a bare cave; still others say it was a tiny, ruined church. The valley's exact location is unknown, although some people say it was a glen known as the Goat's Parlour, which is certainly still there. There was a waterfall down there, beside the ruined building, and a small, clear pool with bushes and low trees all around it. It was an almost inaccessible place; if it was indeed the Goat's Parlour, then it was supposedly used by outlaws during the 1690s and early 1700s.

'There was a small and extremely steep trail down into the glen; many a rider would have turned back at that point, but Sir James urged his mount along it. He wanted to wash himself and give his mount a drink in the pool at the lower end, you see.

'As his horse was drinking and he was refreshing himself at the pool, Sir James was suddenly attacked from behind. At first he thought it was some wild animal that lived in the glen; but, as he fought back, he realised that it was a woman. She seemed to have come from somewhere nearby – maybe from among the ruins of the church, or from a cave close to the waterfall. Anyway, he somehow managed to restrain her; and when he looked at her, he realised that she was the most beautiful woman he'd ever seen, even though she was as wild as any animal. And she *was* beautiful: old portraits of her show a high, fine bone structure, almost Oriental, and long raven hair falling about her shoulders. But it was her eyes – dark, limpid pools in which a man might lose himself – that captivated everyone who saw her.

'Her hands – which he pulled from about his throat – were fine, almost ladylike, although they'd been chafed by her years in the wild; and Sir James noticed a strange symbol just below the base of her right thumb. Later he was told that this was some sort of witch-mark and that it signalled great evil. He should have listened to that warning.

'When she had calmed, Sir James took the strange woman back across the moor to the village of Kilmurry. The people there knew all about her, and they feared her greatly, for she was supposed to be a witch and the daughter of the Devil himself. They told Sir James that she was a demon, and that she would only bring bad fortune to him and his people, but he took no heed of their warnings and brought the strange woman home with him to Drumlane Abbey. And that was how Lady Alice Killigrew came to Bantry.

'Yes, that feral creature eventually became Sir James's wife and mistress of the Abbey. At first she was very wild, like a caged animal, and it's said she even tried to kill Sir James a couple of times. He kept her locked up in one of the rooms of the Abbey, and gradually, over the months, he tamed her. No one knew where she had come from or who her parents had been; nor could she tell them herself, for she spoke in an odd language that sounded very much like Gaelic but wasn't. She had a few words of Irish and English, but the expressions she used in these languages were so blasphemous that they couldn't be repeated in Christian company.

'And yet Sir James continued to keep her at Drumlane Abbey (it is reasonable to suppose that old Sir Desmond was dead by this time), and as the months dragged past she began to quieten down. She learned English and became more civilised in her ways. As she did so, her beauty seemed to increase. Sir James found out that she had no name – at least none that she would tell him – and so he called her Alice, after the wife of the famous pirate Henry Killigrew. She seemed to like the name well enough, and kept it till her death. Nobody ever found out what her real name was or if she even had one.

'At this time, the Killigrews were at the height of their

power and wealth. War between England and Spain was brewing, and Sir Desmond had skilfully played off one sea-power against the other – first granting safe anchorage to the English for a fee, then offering the same to the Spanish. And when the ships were at anchor in a hidden cove near Bantry, Sir Desmond himself would attack and loot them, killing the crews and blaming it on the other side, whether English or Spanish. In this way his clan had increased their fortune to a considerable extent. And Sir James kept up the tradition of piracy and double-dealing that had characterised his father: he accepted honours and revenue from both the English and the Spanish, and secretly attacked them both.

'Alice kept close to him, for she could now take her place in polite society as well as any other woman. However, her wildness and ferocity had been replaced by slyness and cunning. It was said that she was far coarser in her speech than any man and could bring a blush to the cheek of the roughest sailor. She was also said to be sexually voracious, and tradition states that she was having some sort of liaison with Sir James's youngest brother Charles. However, she had long kept an eye on Sir James himself, as he was the official head of the Killigrew empire.

'In the end Charles inexplicably died – some said by poison – and Alice was suspected, but nothing could be proved. She then set her cap at Sir James and stirred him up against his other brothers, creating suspicion and division between them. Thomas, the next brother, was killed in a fight with Sir James over some trifling matter concerning Alice; the remaining two brothers – Robert and William – fled to France to avoid her. William appears to have vanished completely, but we'll hear more of Robert later. As Sir James was now the undisputed leader of the Killigrew clan, he and Alice were married shortly after, and the wild woman from Kilworth Moor became the mistress of Drumlane Abbey.

'If the Killigrews had been bad before, they were worse

now. All sorts of strange ships began to show up in the bay below Drumlane Abbey, and rough and sinister crews came ashore. They began to use the Abbey as their headquarters, drinking and carousing there in a way that old Sir Desmond – ruffian though he was – would never have countenanced. The walls of the ancient building reverberated with blasphemous foreign oaths and clashes of steel as the pirates drank and fought. The cellars of Drumlane were used for storing contraband and pirates' plunder – and, some would tell you, dead bodies as well.

'Sir James himself seemed to have no control over this terrible throng and was pushed further and further into the background of his own affairs. It was Lady Alice who lorded it over the whole assembly, like some awful robber-queen. Not only pirates frequented Drumlane, but highwaymen and local outlaws as well; some of them, it's said, came down from Kilmurry Bridge up on Kilworth Moor, where they were known to gather, and Lady Alice greeted them like old friends. They all sat up in that great barn of a house, scheming fresh atrocities, under the eye of Lady Alice herself. It was said that, when it came to drinking or sword-fighting, she could show any of those louts a thing or two, for her old ferociousness sometimes came to the surface again and it wasn't pleasant to see. What became of Sir James during these gatherings isn't known, but he's supposed to have stayed well out of the way.

'There were many other things said about Lady Alice, too. Some rumours hinted that the most violent rogues were terrified of her, because she possessed supernatural powers; if any of them crossed her, she could wreak a terrible revenge on them. Her alleged witchcraft was the talk of the district, and some people even said that the Devil himself joined in the Abbey gatherings, at the Lady Alice's express invitation. Some of the sailors supposedly asked her to prepare exotic poisons for them, which she did with great skill. Local people also consulted her regarding the future – for she was also said to be a prophetess of considerable accuracy – or for any special potions they required. She claimed to know arts and magics practised by the ancient peoples long before the dawn of recorded history, although how she had acquired them she would never say. Legend, of course, said that she was immortal and that she'd lived up in the Kilworth glen since earliest times.

'But whatever powers she had took their toll upon her, for she rapidly began to lose her good looks. She aged much faster than any other person around her; her raven locks grew streaks of grey and eventually turned an iron-silver colour, while her soft, milky-white skin turned hard and brown and fell into crow's feet. And all this happened over only a couple of years. Lady Alice turned into a raddled hag, withered and wrinkled. Only her eyes retained their old fire, their dark and sinister intelligence. If anything, she became even more vicious and cruel, more blasphemous and drunken – and more dangerous to those who crossed her.

'And what of Sir James in all this, you may ask? Well, he seems to have become a mere shadow – a secondary character in proceedings that were utterly dominated by his evil wife. He seems to have been ill for much of the marriage, although nobody knows exactly what sort of illness it was; old records speak of 'a peculiar ague' or 'a flux of blood', but there's nothing more specific.

'Lady Alice was now the undisputed matriarch of the entire Killigrew clan, and under her dominance, piracy, robbery, smuggling and outright murder increased throughout that stretch of coastline and further inland into Cork. No ship was safe in the waters anywhere near Bantry, nor could anyone travel the West Cork roads with any security. The Abbey itself began to deteriorate, and most of the servants left, leaving the place to the pirates and robbers. From time to time, the authorities would threaten to arrest Lady Alice for one suspected offence or another, but nobody ever did. They feared her magical powers. It was said that she raised violent storms that drove vessels onto the rocks near Drumlane, and that she created sicknesses that swept through the surrounding countryside and did away with her enemies. There were many, many stories about her.

'By now Drumlane itself was nearly in ruins, but that didn't stop the evil ships from arriving and the motley coven of rogues from drinking and carousing there. Things were about to come to a head. On a wild November night, Sir James (who now looked like her son by comparison) challenged his wife to account for her companions and actions. Nobody knows what went on between them, but Sir James was found dead in his bed shortly after. It looked as though somebody had tried to smother him with his own bedclothes, but he'd put up such a fight that the murderer had been forced to strangle him with bare hands. The look of horror on his face was terrible to see. Again suspicion fell on Lady Alice, but again nobody could prove anything.

'As his widow, and in the absence of any brothers, Lady Alice took over the Abbey as his sole heir and continued her evil rule. However, she seemed to be ageing more and more quickly. She had become a shrivelled, mummy-like thing, moving about less and less. Only her eyes were bright and alive with evil. There were times when she seemed to rally a little and get back some of her warmth and colour, but these times were few and far between and didn't last for long.

'It was around this time that children started disappearing from some of the cottages round about. No trace of them was ever found, but it was assumed that they had been captured by the ruffians who inhabited Drumlane Abbey, and carried away on foreign vessels to be sold in faraway markets. However, there were other rumours, because the disappearances coincided with the periods when Lady Alice appeared to rally and regain a little of her youth. Some superstitious people said that she drank innocent blood like wine, and that a little of her looks returned with each sip.

'Even though her body was frail and withering, Lady Alice's dark mind was still alive and full of terrible thoughts. Smuggling increased, and there were several murders in the locality – it was assumed that the victims had accidentally come upon a smuggler's run. One victim didn't die immediately, and was able to identify some of those who had set upon him; he named members of Lady Alice's retinue, connecting her with the terrible crimes. But still nothing was done.

'Then two things happened. The first was that more and more children vanished, and the intervals between the disappearances grew shorter and shorter. Agitated parents began to listen to the superstitious gossip about Lady Alice that was still running around the countryside. Tempers began to rise. Fewer foreign vessels had been anchoring in the bay below Drumlane recently, and the drunken revelry in the house seemed slightly more restrained; there was talk of attacking the place in order to find out what had happened to the missing youngsters. But all this fine talk would have come to nothing if it hadn't been for the second event.

'In the depths of winter, a ship sailed into Bantry carrying Robert Killigrew, Sir James's younger brother, who had fled to France with his brother William many years before. When he had heard of Sir James's death, he had gone to Scotland, amassed an army of gallowglasses, and set sail for Ireland to claim his place as head of the family.

'If anything, Robert was more ruthless than Sir James had ever been, and he was determined that Lady Alice wouldn't stand in his way. On arriving in Ireland, he made himself known to the English authorities as the rightful (male) heir of Drumlane Abbey. They welcomed him and offered their support in any attempt to drive out the rabble who had made the Abbey their home. Robert's band was further strengthened by locals who wanted to know what had happened to their children.

'Late one evening an army descended on Drumlane, utterly surprising the robbers who were lodging there. Whether or not they surprised Lady Alice is another matter; she is supposed to have been waiting in her room on the first floor as her brother-in-law strode up the stairs to confront her. It's said that she screamed at him in a peculiar tongue and pointed a finger at him in an unspeakably ancient sign, but Robert simply struck off her fingertip with his sword and forced her to the ground.

'English and Scottish troops burst in after him, and the wounded Lady tried to raise her hand to issue a terrible spell. With a blow, Robert struck off the hand, which fell to the floor before she could work any magic against him.

'Lady Alice was then taken out and hanged from a crossbeam in the stableyard of Drumlane Abbey, without the benefit of either accusation or trial. The nest of robbers was cleaned out, and Robert (shortly afterwards Sir Robert) was confirmed in his estates and as Warden of West Cork. Lady Alice's body was burned, on Sir Robert's instructions, without any form of Christian ceremony, on a bonfire on the headland near the Abbey.

'Perhaps something of the Lady's influence lingered on, for Sir Robert didn't really enjoy his new estates. He had setback after setback – but he certainly proved himself more vicious than any of his forebears, and under his leadership piracy and smuggling amongst the Killigrews increased to new levels. It's said that he kept the hand of Lady Alice somewhere about the Abbey, well away from sight – where he could look at it when the mood took him – and that this might have been the cause of his misfortunes. Sir Robert suffered from a number of strange maladies, and it was he who was said to have married the mermaid and sired the queer, inhuman children whom he also kept locked away somewhere around Drumlane.

'The hand was still at the Abbey in the eighteenth century. When the famous Argyll highwayman John Malcolm (who, it's thought, was distantly related to the Killigrews) briefly fled to Ireland to avoid capture in Scotland, he apparently visited

Zacharius Killigrew, who was then living there, and was shown
the hand. By this time, of course, the Killigrew empire had all
but collapsed, and the family was practically destitute. Malcolm
was allegedly fascinated by the hand and offered Zacharius
twenty pounds for it. Nobody knows what became of it
afterwards, and it's assumed that it went to Poltalloch in
Argyllshire, where the highwayman was based, and from there
down to England.'

Farrant momentarily paused in his recitation. 'For generations it was thought to have been lost; there were stories that
it was in the possession of some rather sinister people, but
nobody could be sure. And now, as you see, *I* have it! Is it not
a treasure – an occult gem? Who knows what arcane powers it
possesses – maybe even powers from before the dawn of
civilisation! Think of that!'

I must say that, despite Farrant's obvious enthusiasm, the
hand held little fascination for me. I would have preferred to
see the cover of the *Deathbook* of Guido of Tiek, or the scrolls
from the Black Crusade – more historically *substantial* artefacts
– but neither of these was forthcoming. I tried, however, to
show a little enthusiasm for the dead hand.

'Since I obtained the hand, I've tried to research the origins
of Alice Killigrew,' Farrant told me, with a hint of the old passion
of university days in his voice. 'And I'm coming to the
conclusion that she might have been the last survivor of an
old pre-human race, which was supposed to have lived in
Ireland long before the Celts arrived. There are hints about
them in legends – "the People of the Caves", they were called,
because they were supposed to dwell deep underground – but
nothing more. Apparently they were extremely ferocious and
drank the blood of their victims in order to sustain a kind of
immortality. The earliest Celtic kings made war on them and
drove them into the depths of the earth, and soon only stories
about them remained.'

I had heard some of these tales – hints of such a race

appear in Brannigan's *Ancient Myths of Offaly and Tipperary*, and in Lady Duffin's *Strange Tales from the West of Ireland* – but I had always dismissed them as largely unsubstantiated folk myths. Was Farrant suggesting that these old legends were in some way true, and were actually connected to Irish families?

'Of course,' he added, 'that's only a speculation. There's no real proof of her origins.'

'And what eventually became of the Killigrews?' I asked, trying to show at least some enthusiasm. 'Are they still around Bantry?'

Farrant shrugged. 'By the time John Malcolm came to Drumlane, around 1780, they were all but destitute, and most of the family was scattered throughout Ireland. Their piracy and smuggling concerns had practically collapsed, and a lot of other families refused to have anything to do with them. I gather that Zacharius Killigrew owed a great deal of money around the countryside, and neither he nor his descendants could pay it back.

'Drumlane had all but fallen into ruins and there was no money to repair it. When parts of it became positively danger-ous to live in, the family moved away and the name died out in the area. The old house fell down long ago; the title of Warden of West Cork still exists, but nobody claims it. It's said that the family became tinkers and gypsies and still wander the roads of Ireland, and that it all came about through Sir James's involvement with the woman of Kilworth Moor.'

Farrant finished with a kind of self-satisfied smirk, and looked at the withered hand in the box in front of us. There was a momentary silence.

'Quite a story!' I admitted. Was it my imagination, or a trick of the poor light – or did the hand flex itself, suddenly and fleetingly? Just for a moment, I had the distinct impression that the tissue paper in which it lay creased and bunched slightly, and then was smooth again.

Farrant gave no sign that he had seen the supposed

movement. 'I have to admit that putting that tale together has taken up most of my time and kept me away from the paper I was writing. But it's a really fascinating thing, don't you think? The pride of my collection!'

His focus suddenly changed, as it so often did. 'But I've other things stowed away in the house that I'll show you....' At last, I thought, I'll see the *Deathbook* cover and the scrolls! 'Not today, though. Let's put this away for now.' He opened the drawer of the untidy desk and replaced the box. I noticed that, whether deliberately or through carelessness, he didn't close the drawer all the way.

'The hand was blamed for all sorts of mischief against the Killigrews,' Farrant added, as he ushered me from the room and back into the shadowy corridor. Behind me I heard the click as he switched off the light. 'For instance, a strange sickness seemed to haunt the family when they lived in Drumlane. No doctor could determine what it was; it was said to be some sort of plague that Lady Alice had brought down with her from Kilworth Moor. One of the stories says that it was because of the sickness that the Killigrews left Drumlane.'

The room behind us was now in complete darkness, but as Farrant turned to close the door after him, I thought I heard something rustle in the gloom beyond. A rat, I thought; an old, decaying place like Innocent House must be crawling with them. Farrant seemed to have heard it too; his hand froze on the doorknob. Then there was silence in the room again, and he resumed something of his old composure – or as near composure as he could reasonably achieve. He closed the door and made his way down the corridor, with me following close behind.

'Do you know anything about the old races of Ireland?' he asked suddenly. 'Especially the ones that were supposed to drink blood? I've looked at Moffatt, but there's not much in it – more on the wolf-men of Tipperary and the like.'

I had to confess that I knew very little about blood-drinking races in ancient Ireland, and Farrant turned the conversation to other matters. Why he had asked such a question, I had no idea.

We went back downstairs, where Farrant bombarded me with questions again and invited me to inspect more pages of his 'monumental paper' – which were no better than the rubbish I'd already looked at. From time to time he added further anecdotes about the Killigrews, particularly old stories concerning Lady Alice, interspersed with questions about ancient blood-cults of the world. We finished the morning by discussing some of the more bizarre medieval religions, for which Farrant seemed to feel a particular enthusiasm.

The day was heavy, and the dreary oppression of the marshes added a sense of lethargy to my out-of-sorts feeling. Farrant, on the other hand, seemed to gather a kind of hysterical energy as the afternoon passed. I found myself answering his eager questions automatically, talking for the sake of it, without making any real sense. It wasn't as if I could take a walk in the countryside; the day threatened rain, and I had no wish to be caught on the marsh in a heavy shower. So I endured his continual chattering, punctuated only by platefuls of the utter garbage that seemed to be his staple diet.

As early evening drew on, I pretended that I was much more tired than I actually was – I claimed that I hadn't slept well in a strange bed – and suggested an early night for us both. There was no way, I assumed, that Farrant was going to show me any more of his 'artefacts' that day; and I'd made up my mind to leave the next morning, as soon as I could get a train.

Surprisingly, I wasn't really that tired, but I was suffering from a dull, aching weariness that did more to keep me awake than to send me to sleep. The stifling oppression of the old house didn't aid relaxation one bit. I found myself lying full-length on the freezing bed, looking at the damp patches spreading on the ceiling. Apart from the usual creaks and groans of the old house, and the occasional scurrying of a mouse behind the panelling, all was silence.

To relieve the monotony, I got up, went to the bookcase and lifted down the storybook, turning the pages absently. Horror upon horror flashed in front of me as the illustrations passed – a demonic Rumpelstiltskin capered in a shadowy forest glade, where the eyes of monstrous creatures glowed eerily against the darkness; Rapunzel let down her hair to the swain waiting beneath, while from behind her, a claw-like hand reached for her golden tresses; Sleeping Beauty lay in a cobwebbed chamber where rats and spiders held sway, and there was something about her face, perfect though it was, that suggested rigor mortis and creeping decay. From the corners of the chamber, oddly shaped shadows watched. And of course there was the illustration of 'Hansel and Gretel', which for some reason filled me with such fear and loathing.

It was the sinister skill of the artist, I told myself, that added horror to these innocuous fables. I shut the book with a bang but kept it close to me on the bed. For some reason it stirred up memories of the night before, when someone (or was it *something*?) had tried the door of my room. Getting up, I opened my travelling-case and took out a crucifix that my mother had given me and which I often carried with me. I'm not all that superstitious, but something told me I should have the holy thing around my neck that night.

Before I turned in, I did one other thing. I placed a chair tight against the door, directly under the handle, so that it couldn't – so I thought – be opened. Then I lay down on the bed again, with the awful book beside me. Despite all my fears and unease, I must have drifted off into a shallow, uneasy sleep.

I'm not sure at what time I woke again, but it was still early in the night, although the room was in total darkness. I think it must have been the frantic scurrying of the mice behind the panelling that woke me, but I can't be certain, for there was another sound – the noise of the door-handle being slowly and deliberately turned. It was exactly the same sound I'd heard the previous night, but this time it seemed to have more urgency about it.

Instantly, I was fully awake and sitting up in bed, even though I could see nothing in the near-absolute darkness. The handle wasn't moving, but whoever stood on the other side of the door seemed to be having more success than before. Frantically, I strained my eyes against the solid wall of dark, but it remained impenetrable.

'What is it?' I called, hearing my voice low and hoarse. Beads of perspiration stood like raindrops on my forehead.

There was no answer, but again the noise stopped for a second, as if the person in the corridor had paused and was listening with his or her ear close to the door. My mouth was suddenly dry.

The sound started again, this time accompanied by the scratching sounds that I had heard on the previous night. They became more and more frantic, and I suspected that more pressure than before was being used to force the door open. It held for a moment; then, to my absolute horror, I heard the chair that I had positioned against the door fall to one side. Somehow the pressure on the other side had toppled it. The door-handle turned; the door stuck for a moment, then opened inwards, its broken lock rattling slightly.

The light-switch was well beyond my reach; I considered making a dash for it, but somehow my nerve failed me and I simply lay trembling in the dark. I was sure it was Farrant – who else could it be? For some bizarre reason the words of that terrible children's book echoed in my head, spoken in a harsh, sibilant voice – a woman's voice, full of venom and menace:

> *Nibble, nibble, little mouse,*
> *Who is gnawing at my house?*

The mice behind the panelling were going mad, scampering back and forth as if in frantic terror. I waited for somebody to come out of the gloom, but nobody came. And yet I was sure that there was *somebody* in the room with me.

'Richard?' The words came out in a half-croak. 'Is that you? What are you up to?'

Still there was no answer, but someone or something moved in the darkness. There was a faint thud, followed by a skittering motion; I heard a vague scratching of claws, and thought it might be a mouse that had come out from behind the panelling. I tried to jump out of bed and see who or what was lurking in the dark, but my legs felt like water. Whether from sheer fright or from some sort of supernatural thrall, I was riveted to the bed as somebody moved ever closer across the room. There seemed to be a musty smell everywhere.

The bedclothes were gripped and pulled, as though someone was trying to drag me to the floor. A hand – at least, I thought it was a hand – brushed my cheek and searched for my throat. Whoever it was had to be standing very close to the bed, but I could still see nothing at all.

With an immense effort of will, I raised a hand and lashed out. I hit nothing; my fist swept feebly through empty air and fell back onto the bed. Fingers fumbled for my throat again and touched the silver chain of my mother's crucifix. They recoiled, and I realised that whoever – or whatever – it was had taken a step backwards. The mouse scuttled on the floor again – I heard the clack of its claws – and was gone.

Some of the strength returned to my rigid body, and I was able to swing my legs off the bed and put my feet on the floor. I had the distinct impression that whoever had entered the room was retreating as I rose.

'Who's there?' I was still working on the assumption that it was Farrant, although all my senses told me I was mistaken. 'Is that you, Richard? What's wrong with you? Is there something wrong?' I was babbling with fear; I could hear how stupid my questions were.

My fumbling hand found the light-switch, and the room was flooded with light. I whirled round, ready to face whatever intruder stood there.

The room was empty. The mice behind the panelling still scuttled furiously, and the door stood wide open, but I was alone in the centre of the floor. Whoever had been standing by the bed had fled back through the open door.

It could only have been Farrant. Who knows what weird activities his odd studies had provoked, a rational part of my mind whispered. Yes, that had to be it – his nervous energy had tipped him over the edge, and he was probably on the verge of some form of breakdown. This whole house was unhealthy, his studies were unhealthy, the marsh outside was unhealthy....

I went to the open door and looked out. The corridor was in half-light, but there was another light-switch by my hand. If I hoped that the light would reveal a fleeting glimpse of Farrant disappearing round the corner, back to his own room, I was disappointed. The passageway, like my bedroom, was empty. I took a step out beyond the door and looked both ways. The clock at the far end of the corridor greeted me with a steady, almost friendly tick, and a curtain stirred in a tiny draft from the stairs.

Then something moved in the shadow of the wall, keeping close to the skirting board, scuttling down the passage towards Farrant's bedroom. I only caught its passing out of the corner of my eye, but I definitely saw it. At first I thought it was the mouse that I assumed had been in my room; but it seemed much too big and moved far too rapidly, without a mouse's natural wariness. Some sort of huge rat, perhaps? For a second, I imagined it was a spider, for it seemed to have a number of legs – or was that only my impression? Then it was gone, darting behind a large, cracked vase of dried grasses and further down the passage.

I hurried after it but lost sight of it behind a low table.

Still, I could hear it scratching somewhere nearby – a faint rasping sound, like something chewing at the woodwork.

> *Nibble, nibble, little mouse,*
> *Who is gnawing at my house?*

The words of the couplet came back to me with such stunning intensity that I imagined I actually *heard* them being said, in a low female voice, somewhere behind me. I turned; but the passage was, of course, empty. I checked along the skirting board and among the shadows at the end of the passage, but I could see nothing.

The cry made me jump. It was the same scream I had heard the night before, and it came from just around the corner. It could only have been torn from Richard Farrant's throat.

I ran to his door and hammered on it. This time the shout didn't stop; it continued, rising higher and higher in its abject terror.

'Richard! What is it? What's wrong?' I thumped the heavy door until my knuckles bled. I tried the handle; although it was almost as stiff as the one on my own door, it turned and I forced the door in. There was a light – just a bedside lamp on a low table in a corner, but it showed me enough.

If I live to be a hundred, I will never forget the scene that greeted me in that narrow room. Richard Farrant stood beside his dishevelled bed, fully clothed, with a great book open in front of him. He stood bolt upright, and there was a look of utter horror on his pallid face.

At first I thought, in the wan lamplight, that one of the mice – or maybe even a rat – had him by the throat, for there was something under his chin. Then horror piled on horror as I realised that it was a hand. At first I thought it might be the terrible mummified thing that Farrant kept in the drawer in his study, but when I looked at it more closely, I saw that it was a plump, fine-textured hand. It was squeezing Farrant's throat very tightly.

But there was more. Something seemed to be materialising at the hand's end, where it joined the wrist – an arm, connected to the suggestion of a tallish woman. It was little more than a column of smoke; I could just make out the eyes, the cruel mouth, some kind of dark dress. Only the hand seemed real and solid.

Then I realised. The hand wasn't strangling Farrant; rather, it had dug its nails – and they were long nails, like those of the wizened thing back in Farrant's drawer – deep into the weal on his neck, and seemed to be drawing blood from him. Just for a moment, I thought of some kind of suction pump, connected to a water-source, continually drawing fluid up into itself. It seemed to be giving substance to the smoky woman in front of him.

'In the Name of God!' I shouted.

The smoke-column swivelled in my direction, and I saw the face a little more clearly. It certainly seemed to be a woman's face. And, although the mouth was vague and smoky, it seemed to be drawn back into a positive leer of evil.

Something – I don't know what, for I'm not a brave man – seemed to take possession of me. Lurching across the room like a drunkard, I struck out at the hand as I would at some sort of vermin, knocking it away from Farrant's neck. It fell with a wet, sickly sound like a damp towel falling onto a concrete floor, the nails clattering loudly. I realised with a start that this had been the sound I'd heard in my own room – the sound I'd mistaken for the scurrying of a mouse.

As soon as the hand touched the ground, it became the dried, withered husk that I'd seen in Farrant's study. Blood spilled on the floor in a small pool. And, as I watched, the smoke-woman seemed to be dissolving, her nebulous mouth open in a scream of intense fury.

I paid her scant attention; I ran to the bed where Farrant had collapsed. He was apparently unconscious, but I was able to stir him slightly with a few smacks about the face. When I turned back, the cloudy woman had dissipated and was gone. The withered hand still lay twitching on the floor, as if possessed of a life of its own.

'Is ... is she gone?' whispered Farrant, small pearls of blood seeping from between his lips.

I looked around. 'Yes,' I answered. 'It seems to be gone.'

He sank back and closed his eyes once more, blood issuing from the wound on his neck where the nails had entered his flesh. I looked down; the withered hand had somehow righted itself and extended one long finger towards the pool of blood on the floor. It seemed to be drawing the fluid into itself, through its nail, like an animal drinking from a forest pool. The effect was disgusting.

'The bucket!' whispered Farrant. 'By the fireplace. Put the bucket over it! Don't let it get away, or ... or she'll try to come back again!'

I saw a small brass coal-bucket standing by the empty fireplace. Obviously this was what he meant. Leaping across the room, I picked it up, turned it upside down and threw it over the hand, which was already trying to crawl back towards Farrant. The thing was trapped inside it, and I could hear it clattering about and scratching at the metal bucket in its attempts to get out. Farrant fell back on the bed, apparently unconscious.

I stayed awake for the rest of the night, listening to those terrible sounds. After a while, the hand ceased its madcap antics, and silence returned to Innocent House. When I lifted the bucket slightly, early the next morning, the hand lay limp and withered on the floor, just as it had been in the study when Farrant had shown it to me. I assumed that the immediate danger was past.

When Farrant came round, about mid-morning, I learned at least some of the story – the bit that he hadn't told me before. Garret, it appeared, had brought him more than the hand; he had brought him an old manuscript book, reputedly written by Lady Alice Killigrew herself. According to Farrant, part of it described ways to raise souls from the dead, using human remains. Perhaps the old Lady had suspected what might befall her, and had left instructions for her return from the afterlife. She may even have counted on finding someone as gullible as Farrant – who had been drawn to find out more about her, and who had found himself tempted to use the incantations written in her spidery, imperfect script.

The hand, he told me, had always appeared to have a life of its own, but at first it had been no more than a slight flexing of the withered fingers or an occasional involuntary jerk. Farrant had used the hand in a spell he had found in the manuscript book, in order to try and contact Lady Alice. The ritual he had used was very ancient and barbaric, involving the use of human blood – Farrant used some of his own – but it had worked. He had contacted something; he imagined that it was Lady Alice, but it might have been something far, far worse.

And whatever it was had a taste for blood. It manifested itself through the hand: the long nails dug into his jugular vein and drew off tiny amounts at first, then more and more as its form and substance grew. Farrant thought that it was manifesting itself as Lady Alice Killigrew, but he couldn't be sure. The hand itself was becoming more and more active, climbing out of the drawer in the paper-strewn study and wandering about the house. He suspected that it had sought me out because Lady Alice had come to find his blood too weak to sustain her materialisation into this world, and was looking for a new supply. Probably my mother's crucifix had saved me from its attentions.

As time passed, Farrant's worries increased. The hand didn't attack him every night, but its attentions were becoming more and more frequent. He had hoped to raise Lady Alice in order to learn some sorcerous information for his 'grand paper', but now he found himself a slave to whatever was materialising in her form. Maybe, he imagined, she had never existed at all; maybe some ghastly spirit in human form had married Sir James to establish a presence in the natural world. Whatever it was, he couldn't shake it off – that damnable withered hand wouldn't let him.

And yet he couldn't bring himself to destroy the awful thing. It was genuine, of that Farrant had no doubt, and as such it was a relic of a dark and mysterious antiquity that fascinated him. It had him under some form of spell. He had tried to find out about ancient blood-drinking cults, in search of ways to counter the hand's baleful influence – with little success. Every book he'd read treated the subject in a bland, superficial way, giving him none of the answers he sought. One of his reasons for inviting me to Innocent House had been to probe my knowledge on ancient Irish blood-cults.

'I thought that, given your writing on old religions, you might have some answers,' he admitted. 'I was working my way round to asking you.' He didn't say so, but I suspect that he found me just as useless as the books he'd consulted.

There is little more to say. Although at first he seemed to be recovering, Farrant's health broke down two days later and he had to be confined to a mental hospital. He's still there. The hand and the old manuscript book were burned together on a great bonfire at the edge of the marsh. I know because it was I who burned them, alone and well out of Farrant's sight. I don't know if, in his fragile condition, he'd have tried to stop me.

The book burned easily. I carried the hand in the old coal bucket, and waited until the heap of sticks and branches was well alight before tossing it onto the blaze. If I close my eyes, I can still see that terrible thing with its impossibly long fingernails, still trying to climb beyond the reach of the flames, like some hideous spider seeking its prey. Then the branches gave way and it fell into the very heart of the fire. I shut my eyes and didn't look at it again.

In my account of these events to you, I've tried to be as dispassionate as possible. I've tried to set out the story factually, without much reference to my own feelings. I needn't tell you of the effect all this has had on me – the times I wake screaming in the night; the moments when I break out in a cold sweat or my hand starts trembling without warning. Nor need I explain to you that I've come to view the world in a very different fashion. I *know* that below the sane, seemingly normal surface of the world we know lies another, darker, much more sinister realm in which lurk things that we cannot possibly imagine, even in our most fevered nightmares. That has made me distrust things and people. I *know* that death may not be the final end, and that has made me exceedingly fearful. I won't tell you how I can't lift the most innocuous book of children's stories without hearing a voice whispering that awful couplet in my ear. And there are days when I go to visit Farrant in his institution (even though he no longer knows me) and wonder how long it will be before I follow him there. The knowledge I've acquired is almost too much to bear. There are some things that ordinary people should not, must not, know. No, I won't bore you with any of this. I suspect that you may already have guessed it all.

I will tell you, however, that before I finally left Innocent House, I went down to the remnants of the fire to see that everything had been destroyed. Amongst the ashes, something still moved, and I watched in horror as the blackened, fire-scarred hand flexed itself at my feet. Part of it appeared to have been consumed by the flames; and yet the other part still twitched momentarily with a kind of awful life. Then it lay still again – just a withered extremity, scorched by fire.

For some reason that I still can't fathom, I picked it up and took it with me when I left Innocent House. As I write this, it sits on a shelf in front of me, moving slightly, its fingers flexing as though somehow beckoning to me. At the moment, it terrifies me; but who knows how things may change in the future....

MISS O'HARE

You know, sometimes I still think I can hear the sound of her bicycle bell. The sensation usually comes on me when the weather is warm and muggy, just like the days of that summer almost forty years ago. And if I close my eyes, I can still see my father, bowed over, working in our rock-patch of a garden, trimming the edges of sunburnt grasses or digging up weeds with a trowel. At the sound of the bell, he would always straighten up and courteously raise the old tweed hat that he kept for gardening. 'Good morning, Miss O'Hare!' he would call; but she would be gone, hurtling past our low, crowded house on that rickety black bicycle of hers, away into the heat-haze. If she replied to his greeting, her response was lost in the distance.

I knew very little about her in those days. Miss Mary O'Hare. A spinster, living alone in a small cottage further along the narrow country road that ran past our house. Her place would have been much too small for a family like ours (of course, there were nine of us at the time, including Father and Mother) – but then, she was a solitary creature and, said Father, 'far too fond of her own company'. And he was right: she wasn't a sociable person at all. She never encouraged anybody to call on her, the way neighbours did in our area of Wicklow, and whenever any of us children gathered near her gate, she would come out and chase us away with a brush. Although I don't think she'd ever set foot inside Miss O'Hare's cottage, my mother still called it 'dark and poky – a spinster-woman's place'. She might have been right, as well.

It was difficult to tell what age Miss O'Hare was. As a boy
(and you must remember that I was only about nine at the
time), I thought she was very old – maybe thirty or even forty.
She was probably as old as Father, and I knew he was nearly
fifty. If I remember her rightly, she was one of those people
who seem ageless. Perhaps it was her build that made her so,
for she was small and light – my father called her 'a fragile
bird'. She was very, very pale; this paleness was accentuated
by her strawberry-blond hair, which was crammed under a
broad-brimmed straw hat that she wore in all weathers, and
by the redness of her lips. Yes, I think it's her lips – they were
so unusually red – that I remember most; her lips and her
bicycle. It was a big, black butcher's bicycle – a man's bicycle,
with its bar removed so that she wouldn't have to lift her leg
to get onto it, but it was far too large for her to get onto anyway.
It made her look all the more frail and insignificant, as she
struggled to push it uphill and then sailed down the other
side, almost out of control, holding onto her big hat to keep it
from blowing off.

Even back then, I knew a little of Miss O'Hare's history.
Although she looked like a schoolteacher – neat, prim, ordered
– she had never stood in front of a class. I heard Father say she
had been what some very genteel people call 'a paid companion' to old Lady O'Shea, whom I vaguely remember living
at Ardnagapple House. When the old lady had finally died,
Miss O'Hare had bought her cottage from Mick Mooney with
whatever money she had put by. Then, Father went on, she
had 'shut herself away from the world'. And, he sometimes
added, all those long years at Ardnagapple had left their mark
on her; they had made her proud and haughty in her ways.
Maybe she thought she was far too good to be a neighbour to
the likes of us – at least, that's what Mother would say.

To tell the truth, I was just a wee bit frightened of Miss
O'Hare. I know that seems silly now, long years after, but I
was. There was a story going round our school – a little country

school on the very edge of the Ardnagapple estate – that she was a witch who would kill you and eat your bones. She'd killed old Lady O'Shea with poison, in order to get all her money – or so Jimmy Hurley said. When I asked Father about that, he only laughed and said that Miss O'Hare was strange, all right, but she wasn't a murderer – just a poor, lonely old spinster.

'It can't have been easy for her,' he said, with sadness edging his tone. 'Shut up in that big barn of a place up at Ardnagapple, with only the old lady and the servants for company. The old lady was queer herself, and maybe she passed that queerness on to poor Mary O'Hare.'

I knew what he meant. I had only seen old Lady O'Shea up close once – when I went up to Ardnagapple House with Father, who was fixing a window there. I remember her as a small, wizened thing that had to be pushed about in a great wicker chair with iron wheels on it. Father brought me to see her in the great, gloomy front room when he went there to get his pay. I was told that I had to be polite and not say anything, for the old lady was wandering in her mind and might not even know that I was there.

The high sides of the chair made her seem even tinier and more shrivelled. Her skin was so ancient and dirty (I heard my mother saying that she wouldn't allow the servants to wash her) that it had actually turned to a sooty black. She seemed to be asleep, her tiny head lolling forward on her chest, a stained blanket drawn up about her lower jaw, a little linen cap on her head. Her hands, resting on the soiled covering, had the longest nails I had ever seen; they were like the talons of a bird of prey. She looked like something that was long dead – or, at the very least, half-alive.

As we approached, however, she suddenly started up, and the little eyes seemed to flicker with an inner fire. They were very bright, like two tiny coals in the middle of dusty soot.

'Is this one of your children, Seamus?' Her voice was thin

and faraway, like the sound of a little bell ringing in another room.

Father pushed me forward a little. 'This is my second boy, ma'am,' he replied. 'This is Philip. Named after my brother that's dead, God rest him.'

For some reason this seemed to amuse Lady O'Shea. 'God rest him indeed, Seamus,' she cackled – a very unpleasant sound. 'God rest us all.' The red eyes fixed on me. 'Bring the boy forward. I want to see him.' She made a low noise in the back of her throat, a sound between a growl and a whimper. Father urged me forward a little more.

Lady O'Shea strained forward in her chair, and for the first time I saw her face clearly. It was long and narrow and cruel, with a maze of lines and crow's-feet under its covering of grime. She smelt of must and urine. The hands on the blanket fluttered like diseased moths, and one of them stretched out to touch my cheek. Instinctively, I drew back; the long, jagged fingernail grazed my skin, drawing a small ruby of blood that was gone almost as soon as it had appeared. Her touch was cold and dry, like that of a reptile.

'So young!' murmured Lady O'Shea. 'So young! So unspoiled!' And she fell back in the chair, as if the effort of talking had been too much for her. 'Mary will pay you what is owed you.'

Father touched his cap, and we left that big, shadowy room and went down to the study, where Miss O'Hare gave him his wages. As we left, I could still hear the old lady's voice, sighing like the wind in the branches of a bush: 'So young! So young!'

That was the only time I ever saw Lady O'Shea up close. It had been one of her better days. Later, Father told me that she was almost one hundred and five years old, and that her mind was failing. Sometimes she didn't know him at all – although when it came to money, he added with a laugh, she was as sharp as a new pin. I often thought, after the old lady died, of Miss O'Hare alone in that great rambling house, with only that mad, wasted little thing for company. Mother said that the old lady slept most of the time, but there must have been days when Miss O'Hare had to attend to her and listen to her incomprehensible ramblings. No wonder she'd become strange in her ways.

If Miss O'Hare had one friend, it was Mrs Scullion. In many ways, the two of them were direct opposites. Miss O'Hare was small, pale and frail; Mrs Scullion was a big, loud, bosomy woman with a hearty laugh, huge, red, workmanlike hands and a faint black moustache on her upper lip. She had been a cook or something similar at Ardnagapple House, although Mother (who had strong opinions on just about everybody) said that she never did much cooking or baking because old Lady O'Shea ate so little. Unlike Miss O'Hare, Mrs Scullion didn't actually live at Ardnagapple, but came and went more or less as she pleased. I think she did some laundry there, too, but (said Mother) *that* never stretched her, because Lady O'Shea never washed herself at all and put on clean clothes very infrequently. Mrs Scullion, Mother confided in anyone who'd listen, was more than a little work-shy – you had only to look at her own untidy, dirty house to see that – and a little bit too fond of strong drink; no wonder she was jolly all the time! If there'd ever been a Mr Scullion, he was no longer in evidence. Uncle Christy once mentioned that Mrs Scullion had been a widow-woman long before she went to work at Ardnagapple House; other than that, I never heard her husband spoken of at all.

In the ancient, mouldy confines of Ardnagapple, big Mrs Scullion and little Miss O'Hare had struck up a sort of friendship that lasted long after both of them had left the place. I truthfully think that Mrs Scullion was the only person to set foot in that tiny cottage when Miss O'Hare lived there, and sometimes the pair of them could be seen wandering along the local laneways, late in the afternoon, talking very earnestly together. Maybe they were remembering their days at Ardnagapple and how

difficult it had been to work for old Lady O'Shea. In spite of
Mother's comments about her, and even though I'd very little
to do with her, I quite liked Mrs Scullion; she was always so
loud and cheery.

✣

During my ninth year, County Wicklow experienced a glorious
summer. The sun seemed to shine all the time and the days
were very long and drowsy. We children had a wonderful time,
playing through the fields or splashing in the rivers to keep
cool.

That was the year that old Lady O'Shea died. She was one
hundred and eight years old, people said. Towards the end
she'd become very strange. She'd always disliked the sunshine,
and she reacted to our wonderful summer with an almost
venomous hatred, insisting that all the shutters in the big house
be closed tight and that all the mirrors be covered over. Within
a month, however, she was dead.

I remember her funeral very clearly. It was the largest one
there'd ever been in our part of Ireland – like a state funeral;
after all, she was the nearest thing we had to local aristocracy,
and everybody wanted to be seen there. All the locals turned
out and Mother had a field day, criticising everyone she saw
or whispering about their family secrets. If Lady O'Shea herself
had any relatives, none of them attended; it was only her
tenants and neighbours who crammed into the chapel to see
her off.

The priest, Father Heaney, spoke only a few words about
her – which was strange, considering that it was a grand
occasion and that Father Heaney was known for his long
sermons. Still, I was glad that we didn't have to listen to his
high, droning voice recounting the parable of the rich man
and Lazarus (which was his favourite at funerals) for too long.
While he was speaking, I looked around the various pews and

saw Mrs Scullion, looking unusually grave, seated beside Miss O'Hare, whose face was covered by a heavy black veil. She had laid aside her straw boater for a wide-brimmed black hat that made her look impossibly old. Every time Lady O'Shea's name was mentioned, Miss O'Hare would lift the veil slightly and dab at the corner of one eye with a lavender handkerchief, or else grip the ornamented edge of the pew.

The day of the funeral was dark and overcast, although the weather had been splendid until then. Lady O'Shea was laid in the big family vault at the edge of the church grounds. Thinking back, I remember Father standing with my Uncle Christy and Uncle Johneen at the cemetery gates, having a quiet smoke. All three of their faces were unusually earnest.

'A big funeral,' Uncle Christy said. 'They must have all come to make sure that she was in the clay.'

'And that she stays there,' Uncle Johneen added. 'Well, that's the last of them now. The O'Sheas of Ardnagapple – a black line if ever there was one.' He looked directly at Father. 'I've heard that some of them can sometimes rise again if the time is right – God between us and harm! They say that her father, old Sir Manus O'Shea. ...' And he made a curious sign with the first and last fingers of his right hand, in the direction of the burial vault, and said no more. Father looked anxiously down at me.

'Aye, I heard that too,' ventured Uncle Christy. 'I wouldn't put it past the oul' beldam –'

Father caught his arm. 'That's only an oul' superstition, Christy,' he said, with an edge to his voice. 'Put about by them that hated the O'Sheas. And it doesn't fit the pair of you to be repeatin' it. Oul' Lady O'Shea was always good to the people round here. She was always good to me and mine.' He looked down at me again. 'And neither you nor Johneen'll repeat it here to frighten the child. I thought you'd have had more sense, Johneen, with children of your own.'

He hunted in his pockets for a threepenny bit. 'Now, Philip, run along to Patsy Dargan's and buy yourself some sweets.'

As I went, I looked back once; the three men had drawn in around the cemetery gatepost and were deep in some sort of serious conversation. Seeing the looks on their faces, I was glad I was going to Dargan's shop for my sweets.

After Lady O'Shea's funeral, the sun came back and the weather was gorgeous once again. And yet, there was a sort of edge in the air, all through the countryside. It was as if our neighbours had something on their minds that wouldn't let them relax and enjoy the beautiful sunshine. Even Father seemed a bit nervous, as if he was expecting something unpleasant to happen – something that never seemed to come.

And, of course, there were stories. At school, Jimmy Hurley told us that his grandfather Dan Coyne had said that Lady O'Shea wasn't dead at all, but might rise like a ghost at any time to terrorise the country. He said that her father, Sir Manus O'Shea, had roamed the area long after he was dead, peering in at the windows of houses and terrifying the people living there. A brown, shrivelled thing he was, with long nails and sharp, pointed teeth (Jimmy relished this description immensely). That was what Jimmy's grandfather had told him – but everybody knew that Dan Coyne was a bit soft in the head and was forever making things up. So I paid the story little heed.

At first, Miss O'Hare continued to live at Ardnagapple House on her own. Lady O'Shea's death must have hit her very hard; whenever Miss O'Hare's name was mentioned, local people commented on how pale and wasted she'd become. Her life at Ardnagapple had become even more isolated. She kept the shutters of the old place tightly closed, and ventured out even less than before – she hardly even went out to see Mrs Scullion. Uncle Christy was forever talking about her, and sometimes I thought he might secretly have an eye on her, even though she must have been far older than him and, anyway, he had been walking out with Maureen Sullivan for years.

'Mary O'Hare looks very unhealthy,' he'd tell Mother when he called by. 'I wouldn't like to be shut up in that big barrack of a house on my own. She still keeps the shutters closed, even in this weather. It can't be good for her; no wonder she's pasty-looking. Especially with the old lady lying ....' He would stop when he mentioned Lady O'Shea, for Mother would give him a warning look that flitted to us children and then back to his face, telling him to be quiet.

'Now, Christy,' she'd say lightly, 'we'll have none of that oul' nonsense in this house. Do you want to be frightening the children altogether?' And Uncle Christy would smile ruefully and change the subject. I think he was hinting at some secret thing that was being quietly talked about in the countryside – something to which we children were not privy; something that underpinned the widespread sense of unease that seemed to take away from the splendid weather.

Around this time, Mick Mooney took a serious stroke and went to live with his daughter, fifteen miles away, leaving his little cottage standing empty. With whatever money the old lady had left her, Miss O'Hare made Mick an offer for the property, he accepted, and she moved in there. Ardnagapple House was closed up and left to rats and shadows.

✢

The summer drew to a close. As autumn approached and school loomed once more, my brothers and I spent the last days of the holidays playing cowboys and Indians through the forest lanes near our home. We were soldiers, we were pirates, we were explorers and pioneers in a new country, we were anything our imaginations could possibly conceive.

Late one afternoon, my elder brother Martin and I set out on an expedition to explore the grounds of Ardnagapple House. Of all my brothers and sisters, Martin was my favourite, the one I played with the most. Bridget and Therese were in their teens, far too old to be interested in our games; Peter and Kathleen were just seven and six, much too young to play with us; and Tim was only a baby. But Martin was eleven – just two years older than me – and he was my regular partner in crime; most of the time we were inseparable. That summer, he had been reading a book about intrepid missionaries who had ventured into the upper reaches of the Congo River in Africa, and the overgrown grounds of the old house closely resembled (or so we thought) the lush tropical jungle of the stories. Trudging through the thick surrounding woodland, we suddenly emerged in front of the house itself.

Ardnagapple House was a big, awkward, sprawling place, built of frowning dark-grey stone, with high, narrow windows blinded by shutters. There were high peaks and crow's-foot corbels and insets where the slates came down like beetling brows, giving it a forbidding aspect. I think it had originally been a large farmhouse, to which wings had been added sporadically, giving it a queer, lopsided appearance that added to its air of menace. Its façade was overgrown with ivy of various hues, ranging from deep red to pale green. What gardens there had been were in ruins, overrun by a riot of weeds.

But, for two boys, it was a heaven to explore. In an instant we ceased to be jungle-explorers and became ghost-hunters, like *Maxwell Hawke – Sleuth of the Supernatural* in Martin's favourite comic book. We ventured around the dark walls, peering in at the grimy windows and seeing nothing. Jimmy Hurley had told us that the ghost of old Lady O'Shea still travelled the night-black corridors of the house in her wicker wheelchair, and the delicious terror of actually seeing her appealed to us both.

In a small garden enclosure, we came upon the statue of a satyr – half-man, half-goat. It stood, broken and festooned with creepers, above the remnants of a dry, forgotten pond. As I approached it (Martin was still some way behind, probing at

a strange niche in the garden wall) I thought I saw it move –
or, at least, the creepers did. I stopped and stared; a large grey
cat darted out of the creepers and was gone, without a backward
glance, in the direction of the house. It was a huge, glossy-
coated thing, and the suddenness of its appearance must have
made me cry out; in a moment Martin was by my side, asking
me what was wrong. I told him it was nothing – just a damn
cat.

We moved on to explore old kitchen gardens, filled with
nettles and withered herbs with all their goodness gone. Here,
too, were the skeletons of former greenhouses, their glass
smashed; beyond these, a peeling door set into a high wall led
(we supposed) into a back yard, but it steadfastly refused to
open. From the top of the wall, the grey cat watched us
momentarily before jumping down on the other side, out of
our sight.

We contented ourselves with pressing our noses against
several downstairs windows. We saw only closed shutters, and
a couple of empty rooms with large, sooty fireplaces. We could
almost smell the stink of mould and damp through the glass.
A couple of times we came upon broken windows; we could
have actually gone into the house, if we had been careful.
However, both of us hung back. Maybe we were afraid that we
would meet Lady O'Shea guiding her chair through the lightless
corridors. And in my mind's eye, I thought that I could see
inside the old place without actually crossing its threshold –
the great staircase that led down into the hallway; the shadowy
reception room, with its marble fireplace and the mounted
heads of long-dead animals glowering down from the walls;
the twisting corridors along which the ghost travelled in her
wicker chair.

We explored further but found little of interest – only more
shuttered windows and doors barred against us. And yet I had
the distinct feeling that we were not alone, that somebody
was following us, watching us from among the tangled growths.

A couple of times I turned quickly, but I saw nothing – except sometimes the great grey cat, which darted out of my line of vision, behind a buttress or under a bush. Martin had the same sensation – although he never said so until much later – and when he tired of our exploration, he was more than anxious to get home.

As we left the old house, heading back into the parkland around, I looked back. Just for a second, I had the impression that there was a face looking down at us, watching us go, from one of the unshuttered windows of an upper storey. It was too far away to see properly, and it might have been nothing more than a reflection of the late-afternoon sky; but it looked like a face, all right. And, although it was very indistinct, I had the impression that it was the face of Miss O'Hare. I never mentioned it to Martin – neither the face nor my strange feeling that something followed us from that falling house to the very edge of the grounds. It was probably all in my imagination.

It was some time later that I told Father about our exploration of the grounds of Ardnagapple, and his reaction was certainly not what I'd expected. We'd been working in one of the fields near our house, and we'd hunkered down behind a roadside hedge for a mug of tea and a sandwich. When I told him, Father set down his mug on the ground between us, and I saw that he'd gone deadly pale and that his hand was shaking a little.

'You must promise me, Philip, that you'll *never* go up there again on your own,' he said solemnly. 'Not without me or one of your uncles with you.' And, although he didn't think that I saw him, he made that same curious sign with the first and last fingers of his right hand that I'd seen Uncle Johneen make on the day of old Lady O'Shea's funeral.

'Did you go into the house itself?' he asked quickly. I shook my head, stunned by his reaction. He murmured something like 'Thanks be to God.'

The grounds were dangerous, he went on – there were old

cellars, wells and coal chutes into which children might fall –
and the house was more dangerous still. It was filled with rats
– rats that would bite. I was about to tell him about the cat
we'd seen, but he was already reminding me about my cousin
Charlie Lynch, who'd been bitten by a rat when he was working
in an old stone barn on the edge of the Ardnagapple estate.
Nobody had seen the rat, but it had given him a fearful bite on
his hand. Afterwards Charlie, who was a big strapping boy of
seventeen, had been very ill; he had faded away to nothing.
He had died shortly afterwards. Father had gone to his funeral,
but none of us had been allowed to attend, which I thought
was very strange; he was our cousin, after all.

Father spoke more quietly and earnestly than I'd ever
known him to before. He said he'd have a word with Martin,
too. As he was speaking, we heard the sound of a bicycle bell
on the other side of the hedge, and we knew that Miss O'Hare
had gone hurtling past on the road beyond. I have to say that
the thought of her being so nearby at that moment unnerved
me a little. We went back to work in the field; Father never
spoke of the incident to me again, but I knew I'd upset him
somehow.

A few evenings later, Martin and I cycled over to Jimmy
Hurley's house to buy eggs from Mrs Hurley. The Hurleys were
distant relatives of ours, but I've a feeling that Mother disliked
Mrs Hurley, who she always said was 'far too superstitious for
her own good'. Anyway, it was always us children who went
to fetch the eggs – never Mother.

Not that we minded, for the Hurley house was always great
craic. Jimmy's grandfather, Dan Coyne, lived with them. He
was an old, old man, who was sometimes wandering in his
mind, but he knew great stories about the countryside. He'd
been arrested by the Black and Tans; he'd shaken the hand of
Michael Collins in West Cork; he'd been involved in sheep-
smuggling and poitín-making; and he would tell us tales about
it all.

But it was at ghost stories that Dan excelled. When the mood was on him, he would regale us with stories about Saucer Eyes – a dog with eyes as big as saucers, who walked lonely roads and was said to be the Devil himself – or about the Coshta-bower, a terrible coach that carried the souls of the dead to hell, travelling so quickly that it set fire to the roadside bushes. His wild old-man's eyes would light up as he sat beside Mrs Hurley's smoky fire and told us open-mouthed children tales of banshees, goblins and night-walking spirits. That evening he told us a story that, although it had little to do with Ardnagapple House, coloured my view of the place forever and hinted at things to come.

The tale concerned a lone widow-woman who lived in the hamlet of Ballyhoran, about fifteen miles distant. Late one evening, she looked up from her work to see a strange face peering in at her window – a dark, shrivelled, hairless face, looking directly at her.

'She heard the tap-tap of its long fingernails on the window-pane,' went on old Dan, sucking on his pipe, 'and, by God, it was trying to get in at her. She said it had the face of an Egyptian mummy, the sort she had seen in books – all withered and puckered in on itself. But it was the eyes that caught her attention. Like burning coals, they were, plucked from the very fires of hell and set deep in that terrible face. And as she watched, the thing became wilder and wilder, throwing itself at the window to try to get in to her. She tried to scream, but no sound came to her throat. She just stood there, frozen in fright.' By now the old man had us all in the palm of his hand.

'And then the glass broke and the thing came in, flowing across the windowsill like a shadow. It was in the kitchen, and it fastened about her neck like some wild animal. She said it was dressed in a filthy, ragged robe, like a winding sheet. It drew its lips back and bared long, animal-like teeth, ready to sink them into the base of her neck.'

We all sat forward, badly frightened but fascinated all the

same. 'At last she found her voice and let a long, long scream out of her. It brought her brother, that was lodging with her, from the next room. He snatched up a stick from the fire and pushed it at the thing. The creature turned with a great hiss, like the sound of steam from a boiling kettle, and was gone over the windowsill again and out into the night.' Old Dan took a long pull on his pipe. 'When they went outside, there was no sign of the thing that had threatened the woman; but her brother had recognised the wizened face of it. It was old Sir Manus O'Shea, him that lived at Ardnagapple House long years before. The next day the brother got up a party of men, and they made their way to the old burying-vault of the O'Sheas and –'

He was interrupted by Mrs Hurley bringing in lemonade for us and a glass of poitín for himself. 'Now, Father,' she said, 'don't be terrifying the children with your oul' stories. You'll give them bad dreams.'

The old man only laughed and forgot the rest of his tale. We never heard what the man from Ballyhoran and his companions had done at the grave of Sir Manus O'Shea.

'A bad family, they were – the O'Sheas of Ardnagapple,' Dan Coyne murmured to himself as he sipped from his poitín glass. 'All dead. Old Lady Margaret was the last of that bad line – pray to God that she stays in the clay!' And he wandered off in thought, the way old men sometimes do, and we heard no more. Later he told us another story, about the Black and Tans, but he never mentioned Sir Manus O'Shea or his family again. Old Dan Coyne was wandering in his mind, Father told us afterwards, and anything that he said wasn't to be trusted.

Mrs Hurley's prediction of nightmares, however, seemed to be coming true: I had recently started to dream about Ardnagapple House. I hadn't been sleeping well for some time, and gradually visions of the ancient pile had begun to torment my nights. In the dreams, Martin was always there; together we would run through the overgrown woodlands, pursued by an indefinable, menacing *something* that we never saw. Sometimes I thought I heard the squeak of a wicker chair behind us, or the rumble of iron wheels bounding across heights and hollows in the uneven earth, and I thought that whoever or whatever followed us might have something to do with old Lady O'Shea. Sometimes Miss O'Hare was also in the dream, rising out of the dreary woodlands like some phantom, her right hand clutching the awkward straw hat to her head. 'So young!' she would say mournfully, in a faraway voice that didn't sound like her own. 'So fresh!' And she would lift her left hand to show me that the nails had grown impossibly long, like the claws of a cat. I would always wake up sweating, with the sheets twisted around me.

I was becoming frightened to go up to the Hurleys' for Mother's eggs. As the summer drew near its close and the nights became longer and darker, old Dan Coyne grew much more agitated, and the stories that he told grew wilder and wilder. He told us about bloody gun-battles between Regular and Irregular forces during the Civil War, describing them in such vivid detail that it fairly made our hair stand on end. He told us about grisly murders in the countryside long ago; one in particular, where a simple-minded son killed his family in an especially gory manner, almost turned my stomach.

Only once did old Dan hint at anything mysterious or supernatural.

'There's ghosts abroad in this countryside,' he said, pushing himself up on his stained chair. 'Ghosts that walk even in the daylight.' He thrust his wizened old face close to mine, snot hanging from the end of his beaky nose and falling onto his moustache. 'Have you ever been to Ardnagapple House, Philip?'

I nodded, swallowing.

'It's a bad place. People have died around it. It wasn't the bite of a rat that killed your cousin Charlie Lynch, now was it? It was the bite of something else. Something that was hiding in those old barns, away from the sun.' And he fell into a kind of reverie, as if I wasn't there. 'A bad place, all right ... the O'Sheas of Ardnagapple....' He was making no sense. I left him and stole out into the scullery, where Mrs Hurley was putting eggs in Mother's basket. I believe old Dan never even noticed my absence.

✠

Around this same time, at the end of the pleasant weather, two things happened. First, my brother Martin took sick. One night, he went to bed in good health, and woke up the next morning pale and feverish. Mother thought it was a passing chill – the changing weather was spawning all kinds of sicknesses – and kept him in bed. It would pass in a day or so, she said.

But it didn't. She fed him hot broths and beef tea, but Martin only seemed to get worse, paler and more sickly. There were great dark shadows under his eyes, as though he hadn't been sleeping, even though Mother could hardly wake him up in the mornings. He had always been a robust boy who took an interest in everything, but now he was tired and listless.

His sickness made Father and my uncles very uneasy. Father and Mother said nothing, but I could tell by the way they watched Martin that they were worried. At first, I thought they were simply anxious because he wasn't getting better, but then I started to think it might be something much deeper. They talked together in hushed voices; they took Martin's temperature over and over; and once, when he didn't think I was watching, I saw Father check Martin's neck. Maybe, I thought, he was looking for rat bites, like the one that had killed my cousin Charlie.

I shared a large bedroom at the back of the house with Martin and our younger brother Peter. The girls slept across the corridor from us, and Tim, who was still in a cot, slept in the same room as Mother and Father. The great window of our room looked out over the fields towards Ardnagapple Church, and if I stood on tiptoe I could just make out the slanting roof of Miss O'Hare's little cottage, tucked in at the corner of a low hill. In his bed, poor Martin tossed through each night in a fever, muttering to himself in a low, urgent voice, as though he were talking to somebody – somebody I couldn't see.

The second thing that happened about this time was that a great grey cat started to come around our house. I can't say for sure if it was the same one I had seen in the grounds of Ardnagapple House, but it certainly looked like it. It was a big, fat, sleek thing with a heavy coat, bigger than any of the scrawny cats we usually saw whining for scraps at the back door.

It had a strange way about it – even Father said that. For a start, it didn't come right up to our back door, mewling for food, the way the other cats did when Mother appeared; the grey cat hung back, sitting on the back wall or on a stone, watching her intently. Nor did it run to gather up the old crusts and bits of fish that Mother would throw out; it would wait for scraps of meat and fowl, hurrying to snatch them up with almost indecent haste before other scavengers got to them. And when it was approached, the grey cat didn't bolt away; it moved with a slow, stately air, an air of absolute authority, as if it wasn't in the least afraid of humans. At night, as we sat around the fire, the grey cat would sit on our front windowsill and peer in at us with queer yellow eyes.

I think this was the most unnerving thing about it: the strange, unblinking gaze with which it calmly surveyed the world. Its narrow eyes made the broad feline face appear almost human – and malignant. When it was disturbed, it didn't yowl like an ordinary cat – that high, spitting screech; when Father chased it away, it made a low clucking noise, like a woman's harsh, breathy laugh, that was very disturbing. Thankfully, the grey cat only came around our house a few times, but it was certainly about our door when Martin fell ill. I sometimes wondered if there was any connection between his sickness and the appearance of the grey cat.

There was one other thing that troubled me a bit. For some reason, I seemed to see Miss O'Hare about the roads more and more. As I've said, she usually kept close to her house, sometimes working in her little scrap of a garden, only venturing out from time to time. But now, as the summer came to its end, she seemed to haunt the countryside with increasing frequency.

A few times I met her on the road as I made my way home from the Hurleys'. She was usually hurtling along on that big, awkward bicycle of hers and was past me before she even registered my presence. A couple of times, however, I met her face on: as I was going down the hill towards our house, she was coming up it, laboriously pushing the bike in front of her. On these occasions, I kept well to the other side of the road, my eyes fixed on the ground in front of me, and I couldn't tell whether Miss O'Hare watched me pass by or not. I suspect that she did, for I felt my skin tingle as though her eyes were fixed on me, but I was too terrified to look up. The only other time I had felt such a sensation was when the curious grey cat had stared at me from the stones behind our door. I wondered if Jimmy Hurley might be right; maybe Miss O'Hare was indeed a witch, going about the countryside in the awful guise of a grey cat. And all the while, Martin's strange fever grew worse.

Mother and Mrs Hurley fell out about something – I think it was something to do with eggs, either the price of them or some money owing for them. In any case, I was told not to go to the Hurleys' for eggs again, but to go an extra couple of miles to Patsy Gallagher's. To tell the truth, I was very glad of this, even though it was a longer distance, for I had become a bit afraid of old Dan Coyne. His behaviour and his stories were becoming wilder and wilder. As soon as I appeared, he would grab me by the arm and whisper to me about corpses wandering through the countryside at dead of night, trying to get into houses and eat the people sleeping inside. He said that the old graveyard up at Kilhammond was filled with these unquiet dead, and that they were especially fond of the flesh of young boys. By going to Patsy Gallagher's, I avoided hearing the old man's ramblings, and my days were a little better for it.

At home, however, things were getting worse. Martin was sinking fast. Since we couldn't afford the grand doctor in the town, Father brought the Widow O'Leary over from Fallowvee to have a look at him. She was a thin, stern woman who didn't believe in any of the country superstitions and who would take no nonsense from her patients. She had been a midwife at one time, and she had a great knowledge of ailments and sicknesses; her remedies were seldom known to fail, and she was considered to be far better than any doctor.

She came and looked at Martin, making queer clucking noises over his bed, and fed him herbal broths and beef teas mixed with all sorts of things; but none of them seemed to do him any good. The Widow O'Leary told Mother that he was lacking in blood and that she should get a piece of raw meat, squeeze the blood out of it in a press, and feed it to Martin like a soup. That would build him up, the Widow said. Mother did this, seasoning the blood with salt and pepper; she gave Martin the bloody soup about three times, but he still kept getting weaker. And then Peter started getting sick as well.

I will have to say a word about our bedroom. It was a long, narrow room; the beds were arranged so that Martin slept nearest the window, Peter slept in the middle bed, and I slept nearest the door. The sickness seemed to be spreading back into the room from the window, starting with Martin, then moving on to Peter.... It was all very worrying.

Sometimes, in bed, I could hear Mother and Father talking in low, anxious voices; and late one night Uncle Johneen and Uncle Christy both came round, and they all talked very heatedly for hours. I knew it was about Martin's illness, for I heard the Widow O'Leary's name mentioned – and then, surprisingly, Miss O'Hare's.

My two brothers were asleep, poor Martin's breath now coming in faltering rattles. Slipping out of bed, I went and listened at the bedroom door. I heard Uncle Christy's voice in the kitchen, very loud.

'They say she's still about Ardnagapple House,' he was saying. '*Inside* the house, I mean. It isn't healthy for her to be still about that old place – and it all closed up, too. Dinny Nolan saw her bicycle up against the wall near the front door, *and* he saw her at one of the upstairs windows, peering round the shutter. What does she be doing there? Shut up in that musty, dark place, without a chink of light – it isn't natural. Not after what they say about the O'Sheas, that ...' I couldn't hear the rest, even though I had my ear pressed to the crack in the door.

'That's nonsense.' I heard Father's lower voice. 'It was put about by people who had nothing to do but gossip about their betters. They ...' He said much more, but it was lost in the distance between the kitchen and my bedroom.

'I don't know, Seamus.' Uncle Johneen's voice was the lowest of them all. He was the eldest of Father's brothers and was used to being listened to. 'Look at what they found when they opened the vault and looked at Sir Manus's tomb. I was there, and ...' But, whatever Uncle Johneen had seen, I couldn't hear.

'Do you think that the O'Hare woman ...' began Uncle Christy; but at that moment Mother came out of the kitchen and I darted back to my bed.

Although I wasn't sick, my dreams were getting stranger. They always centred around Ardnagapple House and its decaying grounds. Sometimes I would be running fast over the uneven earth, running away from the rumbling sound of the iron chair-wheels that followed me; pushing through the rotting undergrowth, stumbling over bumps and hollows in the ground. And suddenly Miss O'Hare would appear from among the trees, her arms open wide as if to receive me into a welcoming embrace. 'So young!' she would say, in that faraway voice. 'So tender!' And she would suddenly change into a grey cat and leap at me, making me stumble backwards, away from her razor-sharp claws.

In one dream I was inside Ardnagapple House, running along those long, dark corridors, all of which seemed to lead into that great front room where Father had taken me years before. There were the animal heads hanging on the walls; there was the great wicker wheelchair, still in a shadowy corner, and I could just make out the little bundle curled up in it. Against my will, I moved forward. The being in the chair sat up in a stray shaft of sunlight that came in through the broken shutters. I thought that it was old Lady O'Shea, but I was wrong: the person who sat in the chair was Miss O'Hare, reaching out with her long fingernails.

Then the dream became very confused. I thought I was back in my own bedroom, wide awake. Turning my head towards the window, I saw the huge grey cat seated on the sill, looking in at us all. Martin and Peter stirred fitfully. Then the cat seemed to melt and change, and the face of Miss O'Hare peered in, her thin hands scratching at the glass of the pane as though she was trying to get in. And Martin and Peter were sitting up in their beds, their faces so white that they were almost blue. 'So young!' they murmured. 'So tender!'

The bedroom door rattled as if somebody was attempting to come in, and from behind it I could hear Uncle Christy's loud voice. 'It's not natural,' he was saying. 'Shut away in that big house with the O'Sheas. She must wander about in the dark, for she never opens the shutters. It's not right!' Martin and Peter were rising from their beds, their nails growing longer and longer.

'Uncle Christy!' I shouted; but he seemed to be talking to somebody else, and I heard Uncle Johneen's voice – or was it the voice of old Dan Coyne?

'I remember when they opened old Sir Manus's tomb. I know what they had to do....'

And I would always wake just before dawn, bathed in sweat, with the distinct impression that somebody else had been in the room. Maybe it had been Mother or Father, checking to make sure that we were all right.

As the glorious weather faded, Martin died. There was nothing Mother or Father or the Widow O'Leary could do to save him – he just slipped quietly away one afternoon. It was not unexpected, but nevertheless it devastated us all. Father became sullen and silent. Mother, who never shed many tears, cried for days. Although Martin was the only one of us who had ever really stood up to her, she had loved him very deeply. The rest of us children crept about the house, quiet as mice, and our home had a kind of Sunday feeling every day of the week.

On the day of Martin's funeral, Father and Uncle Christy and Uncle Johneen gathered by the cemetery gates again and talked very earnestly for some time. I went over to them, but they told me to go and look for Mother, so I knew that what they were talking about was extremely serious. I did catch some of the words, but not enough to make sense.

'... the O'Hare woman ...' Uncle Christy was saying, waving his hands about as he always did. '... with the O'Sheas ...'

'Speak to Father Heaney about it, Seamus,' Uncle Johneen was advising, 'or even the Bishop.' But Father waved that suggestion away and said something I couldn't quite hear. Mother showed up then and took me away, but I had seen by their faces that they were very worried.

As Peter got worse, I grew more and more anxious. I kept close to the house, fearful that, if I went out at all, he might be dead before I returned. I wasn't as close to Peter as I had been to Martin, but he was my brother, after all.

Other children in the countryside were ill, too. One of the Feeny girls, several miles away, had gone down with a fever and was like to die; another of the Lynch boys, my cousins, had fallen ill and was getting no better. The Widow O'Leary was never off the roads, tending to them, but her legendary powers seemed to be deserting her, for she made no headway against the spreading illness. So I was very fearful for Peter.

And as I helped Mother about the house, in the dying days of the school holidays, I heard the sound of a bicycle bell and Father saying, 'Good morning, Miss O'Hare,' with increasing frequency. She was travelling back and forth past our house, like some terrible gore-crow, waiting for Peter to die. I became very frightened of her.

☩

Just before we went back to school, Jimmy Hurley (we still played together from time to time, even though our mothers weren't speaking to each other) offered to show me a grand secret. He'd been playing pirates in the field behind his house, and he'd dug up something that he thought looked valuable – it could be buried treasure, hidden in the field since some ancient time. Jimmy wouldn't be any more specific, but he offered to show it to me if I came over to his house.

I hesitated between my desire to see the secret treasure and my fear of meeting old Dan Coyne; but in the end the treasure won out. Jimmy and I hurried back to his house. While I waited for Jimmy to get his find from his room (Mother had forbidden me ever to set foot in the Hurleys' house, and I fastidiously obeyed her instructions), I loitered about the corner of the building, desperately trying to keep out of sight. I was utterly unsuccessful: as I slipped round the side of the house, Dan Coyne's skinny claw suddenly grabbed my shoulder. He had been sitting in the shadow of an open door nearby.

'I was sorry to hear about your brother, Philip,' he said in his creaky voice. 'You must be careful yourself. There's death in this countryside, Philip. It's going about like a shadow. There are things that shouldn't be – things that are dead, maybe – going about even in daylight.'

The old man's mind had clearly gone. 'There's women who can travel about the country in the shapes of weasels and stoats and cats. They're witches, boy! I know, for I read it in an oul' book one time. The O'Sheas of Ardnagapple had that power, and they've given it to others. You're a good boy, Philip, and a good friend to Jimmy, but you're in terrible danger. The O'Hare woman still goes up to Ardnagapple, even though there's nobody there now.' He cackled. 'Nobody living, anyway.'

Then old Dan's mood changed a little. 'Never neglect going to Mass, Philip, and pray with holy purity!' His steely grip tightened on my shoulder, and I felt him pressing something into my hand. 'Take this for protection. Always keep it about you. It was blessed by a bishop – a very holy man. It'll turn back the stoat-women and the walking dead. They're everywhere in the countryside, Philip. It'll keep you safe from the sickness that took away your brother. The O'Sheas of Ardnagapple –'

At that moment, Jimmy came round the corner of the house with his secret find.

'Come on, Granda,' he admonished, for he had no fear of the old man, 'Ma said that you weren't to be out wandering about. Get back into the shade afore the sun gets at you.' And he led his grandfather back into the sheltered doorway and sat him down.

I looked down at my hand to see what Dan Coyne had given me. It was a medal of some sort – probably a holy medal. As Jimmy came back, I slid it into my pocket to look at later.

Jimmy's 'fabulous treasure' was hardly worth seeing. It turned out to be a small, garishly ornamented box, which at first looked as if it might be of eastern origin and might have been used for storing small items. However, it was empty; and when I cleaned away some of the dirt that still clung to it, its base revealed the legend 'Buncrana, Co. Donegal'. I was sorely disappointed.

The medal, however, was much more interesting. It seemed

to be made of bronze and was badly worn. I could just make out the figure of the Blessed Virgin on one side, and on the other the head of a man with an impossibly long nose and a bishop's mitre. There was some writing, too, around the edges; it seemed to be in Latin, but the medal was so badly faded that I couldn't read it. The only things I could make out were the word 'Henricus' and some numbers, but I hadn't a clue what they meant.

I didn't intend to show it to anybody; they would have asked where I'd got it, and I would have had to tell them about Dan Coyne. I wasn't sure what old Dan had meant when he said that the medal would keep me safe from the sickness, but if it would keep away the bad dreams I'd been having, then it was worth holding on to. I kept it in bed with me each night, sometimes closed up in my fist, sometimes under my pillow, in the hope that I would sleep peacefully and have no more bad dreams.

In this, the medal failed miserably. If anything, my dreams became even worse.

Sometimes I dreamed that Miss O'Hare came and stood above my bed, looking wistfully down at me. 'Ah, so young,' she would murmur to herself. 'So young, so full of life, so full of blood....' In my dream, I had the distinct impression that somebody stood behind her, and I strained my eyes in the dark room to see who it was. I thought it might be Martin, watching me with fevered, hungry eyes.

A couple of times, I woke up with the impression that somebody had actually been standing over me, and once I thought that a figure had passed by my bed and gone out the door into the corridor. In fact, lying in my bed, I thought I saw the bedroom door move slightly, as if it had just been opened and closed. However, I didn't get up to look out; I thought it might be just part of a dream I'd been having. I went back to sleep.

When I woke up, it was light. Peter was still asleep, but

his breathing had taken on a queer rattling quality, just as
Martin's had before he died. I suspected that poor Peter wasn't
long for this world either.

Going across to the window, I looked out. There, seated
on the stone wall between our house and Ardnagapple Church,
was the great grey cat, licking its whiskers in the morning
sunlight.

That was the day that my sister Kathleen fell sick. Kathleen
was the second youngest of us all – she was only six. Often I
thought of how I'd imagined somebody passing through my
bedroom door, and I fancied that Miss O'Hare had moved
through our sleeping house and somehow infected my sister
with a witchy sickness, the way that old Dan Coyne had hinted
that some women could.

☦

It had always been inevitable that Mother and Patsy Gallagher
would one day fall out. Patsy was small and narrow-faced,
with a scolding tongue; her husband, Eamonn, was a tall,
round-shouldered man who always had a defeated look about
him. It was said all over the countryside that, when it came to
sharp tongues, Patsy could give Mother a run for her money.
So the two of them fell out. It wasn't over the eggs this time –
it was about something else – but it meant that I didn't have to
go up to the Gallaghers' for eggs any more.

Again, I was grateful, for the road to the Gallaghers' led
past the gates of Ardnagapple House. The gates themselves
had fallen off their hinges long ago and were overhung with
bushes and laurels, which threw shadows everywhere. I was
terrified of the place and used to rush past it on my bike. I
imagined that Miss O'Hare would be lurking among the laurels,
ready to leap out at me, seize me in long, dagger-like claws
and carry me off into the gloomy house.

Since Mother and Mrs Hurley still weren't speaking, the

alternative to Patsy Gallagher's was the Feenys' farm; but this was a good bit away, too far for me to go on my own. As usual, Mother had a solution. Mrs Scullion kept a few hens; she was closer and, I think, cheaper than either Mrs Hurley or Patsy Gallagher. We would get our eggs there in future, Mother declared. This pleased me no end, for I liked Mrs Scullion – even though the road to her house would take me past Miss O'Hare's cottage. Still, if I hurried past, I could avoid being seen by her.

Peter was growing steadily worse. His breathing had that awful rattling sound, and he had a continual fever. Father didn't even bother going to see the Widow O'Leary this time. He and Mother sometimes talked about trying to get the doctor from town, but they never did – they couldn't have afforded him, and anyway, what could he do that hadn't already been done for Martin?

I saw the grey cat lurking along the roadside a couple of times, and I knew that Miss O'Hare had her eye on my brother and that she would kill him if she got the chance. I wondered if my holy medal would save him; but then, it hadn't done too much for me – it hadn't kept my nightmares away. I took it out from under my bed and looked at it. It looked so old and worn that I couldn't imagine it would do much to help Peter. In the end, I put it away again.

Uncle Christy called one evening, with the startling news that he was thinking of getting married around Christmas. He and Maureen Sullivan had been walking out together for as long as I could remember, and Mother used to say that she would never name the day – not while her father was alive and she was looking after him. But now she had, and Uncle Christy was bursting with the news.

But it was another piece of news that startled me.

'They say oul' Dan Coyne's very ill,' said Uncle Christy, almost as an afterthought. 'He's taken to his bed, and they say he'll never see the end of the year.'

Father scratched his head. 'Then he must have been taken ill very suddenly,' he said slowly. 'I was talking to him only the other day, and I saw him sitting at the front of his house just the day before yesterday, talking to Miss O'Hare. I thought it odd at the time, for she never spoke to him before – that's why I remember it so clearly.'

The hair on the back of my neck prickled. Miss O'Hare! Old Dan had talked to her, and now he was dangerously ill. The malign influence of the witch-woman was spreading far and wide across the countryside, gradually defeating anyone who would stand against her. My terror increased a thousand-fold.

Peter grew worse, and so did Kathleen. I asked about old Dan Coyne, but Mother didn't seem to know anything – she kept well away from the Hurleys. The dreams got more and more terrifying. Miss O'Hare and Martin chased me through the dark corridors of Ardnagapple House, and everywhere there was the sound of iron wheels, echoing through the ancient building. Everywhere I ran, doors closed before me, until at last there was no escape....

I woke with the sweat standing on my forehead. The great grey cat was on the windowsill, watching me with an almost human intensity. Or was that part of the dream? I wasn't sure. When I got up, the cat was gone. Maybe it was all my imagination.

My worst day was only a couple of days later. I had been going up and down the road to Mrs Scullion's, over the weeks, and I had always managed to get past Miss O'Hare's cottage. Sometimes I would see her working out behind the house, in her scrappy little garden, but mostly she was sitting by her window, reading a book. People said she had taken part of the great library from Ardnagapple House and piled it up in her narrow little cottage. Dinny Nolan, who'd called at her door one day, said that the place was piled high with books – more than Miss O'Hare could ever read. Why she kept them, I don't know, but she seemed to be reading her way through them, anyway. Most times, she was so deep in her reading that she never noticed me as I went past. That is, until that awful day.

I had passed by her cottage gate and was starting to push my bicycle up the hill towards Mrs Scullion's when I heard her voice behind me.

'Philip Casey!' Her tone was cold and imperious.

I froze mid-stride. Half-turning, I stole a glance behind me, expecting to see Miss O'Hare quite close, her hands outstretched above her head and those impossibly long fingernails menacing me – the classic monster pose, which I'd once seen at the cinema in town.

Of course, she was doing nothing of the kind. She stood in the very centre of the road, looking after me. She had taken off her straw hat, and her fair hair was tied in a bun behind her head. I noticed that it was flecked with grey. She wore a navy print dress and tiny shoes. The fields sloping down on either side of the road made her look incredibly small. And yet, she exuded a chill that frightened me beyond words.

'Philip Casey!' she repeated. 'I want to have a word with you!'

I stopped and turned the bicycle a little, shifting my gaze to the road in front of me. Miss O'Hare never moved.

'I believe you have an old holy medal that was given to you. I'd like to see it.' She stretched out her thin arm in my direction. Although her hand was perfectly normal, I somehow got the impression of long, bird-like claws.

The back of my throat dried up. I didn't always carry the medal that Dan Coyne had given me; at that moment it was at home, under my bed. I wished I'd had it with me, to protect me from Miss O'Hare.

'I … I don't have it with me, Miss … Miss O'Hare,' I stammered, keeping my eyes fixed on the road. I could hardly answer her, for the fear was choking me. 'It's … it's at home.'

My reply seemed to irritate her; she gave a snort and spun

on her heel. When I lifted my eyes from the road, she was gone, back into her cottage. Thanking God for my miraculous escape, I turned the bicycle once more and rushed on up the hill towards Mrs Scullion's.

I must have been pale and breathless, for big, blowsy Mrs Scullion, who'd been working in her kitchen, threw up her hands as I entered.

'Glory be, Philip Casey, you look as if you've seen a ghost!' she exclaimed in her loud, cheery voice. 'Come in and sit down, boy!' And she half-guided, half-pushed me into a sagging armchair in a corner of the room.

Mother was right: Mrs Scullion's house *was* cluttered, untidy and maybe even dirty – but, at that moment, it was the most homely, welcoming place on earth to me. Mrs Scullion gave me a sweetish orangey drink in a cracked china cup, and I drank it down almost in one gulp, while she looked on, rather bemused by my condition.

'What happened to you, Philip?' she asked. 'Did Mike Cassidy's dog make a run at you?'

I shook my head.

Her face clouded slightly. 'Or is it because of your brother Martin? Glory, Philip, I was sad to hear about it, and I know how badly these things can sometimes affect a child. Would you like more orange? And a wheaten scone, maybe? I baked them myself this morning.'

I nodded. Although Mother had told me never to eat anything in Mrs Scullion's – 'Far too dirty a place for wholesome food' – I was glad to have something in my stomach after my encounter with Miss O'Hare. Should I tell Mrs Scullion the truth, I wondered? I'd always liked her, and she was so jolly that it seemed she would listen to anything, no matter how far-fetched.

'It … it was Miss O'Hare,' I began. 'She startled me on the road….'

Mrs Scullion gave one of her bellowing laughs. 'Mary?'

she thundered. 'Ah, Philip. You're easily startled! Mary O'Hare wouldn't hurt a fly. How did she startle you?' She was trying to conceal her mirth behind her faint moustache, but she was laughing at me just the same.

'She ... she came at me all unexpected on the road,' I gulped.

Reaching down, Mrs Scullion put a great mannish hand around my shoulder. Close to me she smelt of polish, grease and sweat – and something else; I couldn't put my finger on it, but it was as repulsive as the other smells.

'Ah, now, Philip, there's no harm in Mary O'Hare. She's just a ... a wee bit strange in her ways. That's what comes of living up at Ardnagapple with only oul' Lady O'Shea for company. But there's nothing in it. She's a good soul really. Even if they say that she never goes to Mass.' She gave another booming laugh. 'Sure an' I don't go meself, and that doesn't make me a bad person, does it, Philip?'

I shook my head, not really knowing what to say.

'An' Mary O'Hare's as good as myself. She's a little mouse of a being – couldn't bring herself to harm anyone. Now, Philip, do you want a wheaten scone, maybe?'

I forced the heavy scone down and had another cup of the orangey dring before straightening myself up for the road home. I resolved to say nothing to either Mother or Father about the incident – they wouldn't have understood, and anyway, they had their hands full with Peter. I kept my resolution.

Every night in my dreams, I ran through the passages of Ardnagapple House, looking for a way out; and every night, I met Miss O'Hare in the darkness. I would wake sweating, thinking that someone else was in the house – that somebody had either stood over my bed or else passed by it on their way to another room.

One night, a couple of days after I'd met Miss O'Hare on the road, I half-opened my eyes in the early morning to see my bedroom door swing shut as if somebody had just left the room. I was sure that I wasn't dreaming. There was a slight chill in the air and, peering out from under the bedclothes, I saw that the window was open a little way. Peter lay in a deep sleep, wheezing and rattling and murmuring softly to himself.

Sliding over the edge of the bed, I went to the door and looked round it. The whole house was bathed in the half-light of the early morning, and, although the night had been soft and balmy, there seemed to be a chill in the air, like the first frost of a winter's morning. I stole forward. The corridor was empty, but the door across from ours had been pushed open a little. It was the door that led into my sisters' bedroom.

Cautiously, I took another step towards it. There was a sudden flurry of movement and something hurtled past me, over my bare foot and into my own bedroom. It was the sleek grey cat.

I turned to go after it, but it bounded through the open window with one leap and dashed into the bushes at the end of the garden. And, as it did so, I heard my sister Kathleen cry out in her sleep. There was a stirring in the rest of the house, and I thought it better to go back to bed.

Kathleen's condition grew a little worse. She still went about the house, but she had grown very pale, her eyes had sunk into her head and she had an irritating cough. Peter was now largely confined to his bed, just as Martin had been before his death.

There were other deaths in the countryside, too – Jimmy Hurley's brother Patrick, little more than a baby; an old man at Ballyhoran (who, in truth, hadn't been well for years); the young Feeny girl. The deaths were widely scattered, but they left a kind of numb and wary secretiveness throughout the whole countryside. People lowered their voices when they spoke of the deaths, and they started visiting each other more often. Any sickness in the district, no matter how small, was greeted with alarm. Father said that many people had stopped going to the Widow O'Leary; when people fell ill, the families just kept to their houses, facing the deaths of their loved ones with a sort of weary resignation.

Uncle Christy never seemed to be away from our house, and sometimes Uncle Johneen would come with him. They would always arrive in the late evening and sit in the kitchen long after dark, talking with Father and Mother, when they thought we children were asleep. I often heard Uncle Christy's voice, rising and falling as though in anger, talking about 'the O'Hare woman' and how 'something would have to be done', and Uncle Johneen's lower tones mentioning 'the O'Sheas of Ardnagapple'. Then somebody would hit the table with a fist, and Mother would tell them not to wake the children. They were all frightened, I think.

A couple of times I passed Miss O'Hare's cottage, on my way up to Mrs Scullion's, but I kept well to the other side of the road. One time, though, I did stop in the shadow of a great laurel bush that grew close to her gate, simply to watch her. She sat by her window, reading the books she'd brought from Ardnagapple House. They were piled on the windowsill and she was skimming through them, picking up book after book, flipping page after page, as though she was looking for something. She was so intent on her own business that she never saw me lurking there.

I wondered why she had taken such an interest in the holy medal that Dan Coyne had given me. She must have somehow learned about it from the old man himself. Now he was confined to his bed, probably because of something she had done to him, and people said he was likely to die before the end of the winter – if he lasted until then. I had never put much faith in his medal – after all, it hadn't kept the terrible nightmares away – but I still kept it, in the little cardboard box under my bed where I kept my football cards, marbles and other odds and ends. Maybe I had been wrong – maybe the medal *was* important....

At that moment, Miss O'Hare looked up from her book –

looked in my direction, as if she knew that I'd been there all the time – and I ran back to my bicycle and pushed it all the way up the hill to Mrs Scullion's as quickly as I could.

Mrs Scullion always cheered me up. Every time I called, she poured me that orange drink in the same cracked cup, and gave me either pancakes or a bun to make the journey home a little easier. Without telling her too much – for I knew that the two women were quite friendly – I tried to hint at my concerns about Miss O'Hare.

'Dan Coyne says she's a witch,' I told Mrs Scullion. Dan Coyne had never said anything of the sort, but it was a good opening.

Mrs Scullion only laughed. 'Dan Coyne's wandering in his head,' she retorted in her loud, hearty voice. 'You shouldn't pay any attention to what he says, Philip.'

She changed her tone a little, becoming more serious. 'He's not long for this world, and people sometimes get strange fancies when they're about to die. No, Mary O'Hare has had a hard life. It wasn't easy pushing old Lady Margaret about in her chair. The old lady had queer ways about her, too, and they seem to have rubbed off on poor Mary.' She shook her head.

'But Dan Coyne says she goes about the country in the shape of a weasel or a cat!' I persisted. 'He says he read it in a book!'

Mrs Scullion gave a sad smile. 'That's only oul' superstition, Philip. And Dan Coyne's only foolin' with you, for I know for a fact that he can't read.' And she would say no more on the subject. That sort of reassured me; but, all the same, I took the holy medal out of the cardboard box that night and put it under my pillow.

Peter died a couple of days later. The effect on our household was beyond words. Mother withdrew into herself, sat in a corner and said nothing, and Father just walked around the garden as if in a dream. Father Heaney called a couple of times;

he said something about it being 'God's will', but I think even he was baffled by the strange sickness that was taking away so many of his parishioners.

On the day of Peter's funeral, we children were sent home from the church early while the adults went to the cemetery. Afterwards, Uncle Christy and my father went to Madigan's pub and came home stinking drunk. Even now, if I close my eyes, I can see Uncle Christy sitting on a low chair in our kitchen, with his cap badly askew, while Aunt Bridie – Mother's sister – tried to sober him up with black tea.

'It's them bloody O'Sheas and the O'Hare woman!' he was mumbling. 'They said that oul' Sir Manus would never lie still in the clay, and Lady Margaret's the same. Either that or she's taken over the O'Hare woman – made her like herself – and it's *her* that's killing the people. Bloody curse of a woman!'

But Aunt Bridie only made him drink more tea. 'None of that language in front of the children, Christy Casey!' she admonished him (Aunt Bridie's tongue was almost as sharp as Mother's; they were sisters, after all). 'And I'll not hear a load of oul' superstition in this house! That'll just frighten the wee ones!' Of course, none of us knew what Uncle Christy was talking about, so her rebuke was wasted.

✟

As the last of the glorious summer passed, the weather took on an overcast, thundery temperament. The days were filled with a sullen, heavy heat, and the nights were clammy, making sure nobody got much sleep. In such weather, Kathleen's condition worsened; and my older sister Bridget, who slept in the same room, began to show symptoms as well. Sometimes I would stand at my bedroom window, watching dark clouds gathering over the hill where Ardnagapple House stood, and I would wonder if this horrible clammy heat could have been created by the witchcraft of Miss O'Hare. I heard Uncle Christy saying that Dan Coyne was near his end, and that the weather was doing him no good.

The sullen heat was matched by a sullenness in my family. Following Peter's death, Father took to drinking more. He hadn't been a great drinker, but now he never seemed to be out of Madigan's or Redmond's of the Hollow, and many an evening he came home staggering. Sometimes Uncle Christy went with him, or Uncle Johneen (although he never really got as drunk as the other two). Mother went about the cottage as if she were in a dream, paying no attention either to Father or to us. She let the washing and cooking slip, and many a time we came in to find no food on the table or no clean clothes for us in the cupboard. She and Father seldom spoke. Something seemed to be eating at my family from inside, drawing the goodness and vitality out of every one of us.

I went back to school. I had always been a fairly able scholar, but now my heart wasn't really in my studies. I couldn't keep my mind off what was happening at home, and I suppose the depression that pervaded the household had affected me as well.

Late one afternoon, I came home to an empty house – well, almost empty. Mother had taken baby Tim and gone up the road to the Clearys, our neighbours (she had lately taken to going up to sit in Mrs Cleary's kitchen, drinking tea and saying next to nothing); Father was stacking turf; my sisters were out – except Kathleen. She had taken an afternoon nap, which, in her weakened state, had extended into the early evening.

Over our house, the sky was dark; heavy rain-clouds swirled in great bunches, forming a huge black fist just above our chimney-stacks. There was a wind rising, too, whipping at my hair as I came into the house.

Instantly, I knew that I was not alone. There was somebody else in the house – somebody besides Kathleen. Despite the heavy weather, the house was chilly, and there was a smell –

like something rotten, left in some forgotten place – that made me wince. I peered into my room and saw that the window was a little open.

Miss O'Hare, I thought. She had come into the house in her cat form, while everybody was out, and was perhaps doing something unspeakable to my little sister.

I rushed across to my bed and took the holy medal from beneath the pillow; then, turning on my heel, I ran to the partly open door of Kathleen's room. Glancing round the door, I saw that I had been right.

Kathleen lay in a sound sleep, the bedclothes drawn up almost to her chin. Seated on her chest was the great grey cat, its head thrust forward as though it was staring into my sister's face. Its pink tongue snaked out, licking at Kathleen's face and neck. Each time it touched her, my sister moaned and moved slightly; the cat simply shifted its position and continued to lick. Oblivious to my presence in the doorway, it suddenly pushed its large head forward and seemed to nuzzle Kathleen.

The full horror of what was going on suddenly dawned on me, and I could keep still no longer. Raising the holy medal in front of me like a sword, I stepped into the room.

'Miss O'Hare!' The words sprang from my lips without any conscious bidding.

The cat turned its head and fixed me with its narrow yellow eyes, drawing its lips back in a venomous hiss. I glimpsed blood on its teeth. Leaping off my sister's chest, it arched its sleek back as though to spring at me.

'I know who you are, Miss O'Hare!' I held up the medal.

She grabbed me from behind. Half-turning, I saw the faded floral-print dress and the straw hat. One thin arm was thrown across my chest as if to protect me. Out of the corner of my eye, I saw that her other hand gripped a large book with a black cover, on which was printed a curious red symbol.

'Throw the medal, Philip Casey. Make sure you don't miss!' Miss O'Hare's voice was high and excited. At the sound of it, the cat sprang, bouncing off the bedroom wall and dashing, quick as a flash, past us and into my bedroom. It was making for the window.

'Quickly!' shouted Miss O'Hare. 'We can still get it!'

She let go of me, and together we ran into my bedroom – just as the cat clawed its way over the windowsill, seeking the open space beyond. Somewhere behind us, I heard Father's voice as he came in from the turf-stack.

As the cat leaped from the windowsill, I threw the medal. It caught the creature high on the back. In the same moment, Miss O'Hare pulled open her book and screamed something – no more than a couple of words – in what seemed to be Latin.

Then the cat was gone; but it appeared to be slowing down as it ran across our garden and scrambled over the wall between us and Ardnagapple. It half-fell off the wall and out of sight.

'Come on, Philip Casey!' Miss O'Hare rushed out of the house and into the back garden, with me at her heels. 'You've done your work! It's up to me now … me and the book….' She was breathless but still running. A rising wind plucked at our clothing with invisible fingers, and the sky overhead seemed to darken even further.

We reached the wall and peered over. My heart stopped.

Mrs Scullion lay on the other side of the wall. She was twitching, trying to rear up, but her eyes were closed and she appeared to be in great pain. Her great fat body heaved and moved involuntarily, as though it was being racked by spasms, and her lips flexed and grimaced horribly.

Still holding the open book, Miss O'Hare said a few more words in that Latin-like language and made the sign of the cross in the air. As if in response, Mrs Scullion momentarily raised one of her hands and clawed at the air; I saw that her fingernails were impossibly long, and that the backs of her big, mannish hands were covered in grey fur, though it was disappearing even as we looked. From under her faint moustache came a thin trickle of blood. At first I thought she had bitten her lip, but then I realised that the blood might be my sister's. Above us, the dark sky grumbled and muttered – but the clouds were slowly starting to disperse.

'I knew it had to be her!' said Miss O'Hare stiffly, closing the book. 'And I knew that her hunger was growing. That's why she came to your house before it was dark, and that's why I followed her.'

She might have said more, but at that moment Father came rushing up to see what was going on. Crossing himself, he knelt down beside Mrs Scullion; but there was nothing he could do for her. She was dead. Later, Father would say that she'd fallen, while trying to climb over a wall, and hit her head on a rock. The doctor accepted that. But I think that Father knew. I think everybody in our area knew.

There is little more to tell you – just a few loose ends to tie up. We had all – and I include myself in this – badly misjudged poor Miss O'Hare. She had a far stronger spirit than any of us had suspected.

For years, in that lonely house, she had somehow resisted the advances of the hideous Lady O'Shea – the last of her terrible line. The old creature had probably known she wasn't long for this world, in that decaying body, and so she'd tried to seek out another body to house her own dark soul. That was how these creatures maintained their long and horrible lives, I heard Uncle Christy say. But Miss O'Hare had managed to keep her at bay; and so the ancient witch had turned on another of her servants, Mrs Scullion, who was less able to resist her evil. Even though she was a big bawling woman, there must have been something in her nature that was weak, just as little Miss O'Hare's was very strong.

Nobody had ever suspected that Mrs Scullion was somehow different, or that she now had the power to go about the countryside in the shape of a cat – a power that had been given to her through the witchcraft of old Lady O'Shea. And nobody suspected that she had the need to drink blood from the old, the weak and the defenceless, just as it's said the O'Sheas had done for centuries – though Mrs Scullion's need was stronger than Lady O'Shea's had been. Maybe such beings become hungrier when they take on a new form; or perhaps it was that, while Lady O'Shea had been small and weak, Mrs Scullion was a huge woman with huge appetites.

But Miss O'Hare suspected. She knew the legends about the O'Sheas of Ardnagapple; and perhaps she noticed subtle changes in her former companion during their long talks – which I think might have become something like interrogations on Miss O'Hare's part. And she had been very fearful, both for herself and for her neighbours. As I said, we'd all badly misjudged her.

Miss O'Hare knew – maybe Lady O'Shea had let it slip – that somewhere in Ardnagapple House there was a book containing some sort of counter-charm against the vampiric evil, but she had been unable to find it. She had taken about half the library back to her cottage, but she still hadn't found what she needed. So she had made frequent visits to Ardnagapple House, exploring every room, until at last she found the volume, in a cranny in one of the attics. Then she set out to confront Mrs Scullion – just in time to save my sister.

There were other questions, too. Where did the holy medal come from, and why did old Dan Coyne give it to me, instead of using it to protect himself and his family? I never did find out where it fell when I threw it, and I never saw it again, though I looked for it. Maybe Miss O'Hare picked it up. I did come across a picture of something that looked like it, many years later, in an old book from Scotland. The caption said it was a commemorative medal struck in the 1500s for Ioannes Henricus (John Henry) McLean, a noted Scottish exorcist and one-time Bishop of the Isles. Maybe one of those medals had somehow found its way to Ireland and been passed down in the Coyne family as a protection against the nearby evil of the O'Sheas. And perhaps, after Martin's death, old Dan saw that this evil was targeting my family, so he gave the medal to me, to guard us against it. I know this isn't much of a theory; but it's the best I can come up with.

And that was all I was able to find out. There are still things that need to be explained, but I suppose they must remain obscure forever. What was the exact nature of the curse that blighted the O'Sheas? Was it something to do with old Sir Manus, or was it much older still? What happened to the mysterious book that Miss O'Hare used — where is it now? I suspect that the answers I want will always elude me.

They buried Mrs Scullion soon afterwards — that is, they buried the thing that had passed for Mrs Scullion. I heard Uncle Christy say that she hadn't really been alive for a long time; her body had only been a shell, occupied by some evil spirit that might once have been one of the O'Sheas. I didn't really understand what he meant.

Mrs Scullion wasn't buried in Ardnagapple Cemetery, but in an unmarked plot well outside the churchyard wall. Before she was buried, Father Heaney poured salt and holy water into her grave. There was some sort of ceremony over the body, which we children weren't allowed to attend; Jimmy Hurley said that Father Heaney cut out her heart and burned it, and he might well have been right. I do know that Father Heaney visited Mrs Scullion's house several times, after the burial, and took away things from it.

Those who had been sick soon recovered — except old Dan Coyne, who died before the winter was out. As far as everybody was concerned, the whole affair was at an end.

But it had left its mark on the area. Father never really recovered from Martin's and Peter's deaths. He continued drinking heavily for years, until the bottle finally got the better of him: he died in hospital, an alcoholic. Mother had died before him, burned out and broken by her anguish.

And the saviour of us all — Miss O'Hare — left the district shortly after Mrs Scullion's burial. Apparently she went to live

with an unmarried sister in County Waterford. Nobody kept
in touch with her. Maybe we were so shocked by the evil that
had dwelt in our midst that we wanted no memory of it. I
expect she's long dead by now.

My sisters both made a full recovery. Kathleen is now a
grown woman, married and living in County Armagh, away
in the North. The rest of us are all scattered – Bridget lives in
England, Therese in County Sligo, while Tim, the baby, has a
family in Hobart, Tasmania – and we seldom keep in touch.
Uncle Christy never married Maureen Sullivan. They fell out
with each other shortly after Mrs Scullion's death; Maureen
married a hill farmer from Kilnahannon, and Uncle Christy
went to his grave a bachelor. Uncle Johneen is long dead, too,
though one of his sons – Matthew – still farms around
Ardnagapple. Jimmy Hurley stayed in the area and married a
local girl. I'm told that he has a family of six and runs the post
office up at Ballyhoran Cross.

As for me, I joined the Jesuits and became a priest – Father
Philip Casey. Maybe glimpsing the true face of evil, and seeing
the damage it can do to decent people, eventually guided me
towards the priesthood – I don't know. Anyway, I served in
the African missions for a while, and then came back to Ireland
to teach and lecture in Dublin. I've been here ever since.

But the memory of that summer when I was nine, and the
questions it raised, have never gone away. I sometimes think
of going back to Wicklow; but what would there be for me to
see? Ardnagapple House no longer stands. Not long after that
summer, it was sold by auction to a property developer, who
pulled it down and built new houses on the site. Mrs Scullion's
house mysteriously burned down and had to be demolished
as well. People said there were things in it that were best
destroyed; but who can tell?

And, even if I went back, who would I talk to? Many of
those who were involved have either died or gone away, and
those who remain probably wouldn't talk. Father Heaney is

long gone; I don't even know the name of the priest who's there now.

A couple of years ago, I did try to find out something about the O'Sheas of Ardnagapple and about what sort of curse might have afflicted them. Admittedly, my research was confined to only three books – Father Harrington's *Notable Families of County Wicklow* (1892), O'Reirdon's *A Brief History of Ardnagapple Church and Its Environs* (1928) and Myles Keating's *Irish Revenants* (1932) – and I found very little. Although all three books briefly discuss the O'Sheas, none mentions either Sir Manus or Lady Margaret (both were probably still alive when the books were written). O'Reirdon hints at folktales about O'Shea ancestors who had made pacts with the Devil or who were rumoured to dabble in Satanic arts, and Keating implies that some of the family might well have been vampires; but these are only whispers and suggestions, saying nothing specific.

And there I let the matter lie. But I have never forgotten that ancient evil from years ago, and what it did to a small, frightened boy in a small and frightened community.

As I write this, it's a glorious day, and late-summer brilliance streams in through the open window above my desk. Familiar scents and sounds drift into the room, and it takes no great leap of the imagination to feel the warmth of the Wicklow sun on my face; to catch the drone of lazy bees competing with the sharp, sudden sound of a bicycle bell; or to hear my father's voice echoing down across the years – 'Good morning, Miss O'Hare....'

CAVAN COUNTY